The Human Builder

From Weakest Link
to
Human Firewall in Seven Days

by Michael Marrano

Copyright

The Human Firewall Builder by Michael Marrano

For more information visit
www.humanfirewallbuilder.com

© 2018-2023 Michael Marrano

Cover by M. Marrano and E. Marrano

Second Edition

Disclaimers

The events, characters and scenarios depicted in this work are fictitious. Any similarities to actual persons, living or dead, or to actual events, is purely coincidental.

The information on this book is for general informational purposes only. The information presented in this book is not legal advice or a legal opinion, and it may not necessarily reflect the most current legal developments. You should seek the advice of legal counsel of your choice before acting upon any of the information in this book.

While the author will try to revise the book on a regular basis, it may not reflect the most current technology, cybersecurity and identity theft developments. The information in the book may be changed without notice, and is not guaranteed to be correct, complete or up-to-date. The author will not be liable for any losses, injuries, or damages arising from the use of the book. The information in this book is provided as is, with no warranties and confers no rights.

Table of Contents

About The Human Firewall Builder

Over the years I have performed many cybersecurity awareness training presentations for companies and I learned the best way to get anyone's attention, get them thinking and get them discussing cybersecurity is to make it relatable. For centuries stories have been used to entertain, educate and inspire.

Another practical educator is life experience and mistakes are often the best teachers of all life experiences. Learning through experience such as mistakes can be hazardous such as learning to be a better driver by going through stop signs and potentially getting into car accidents.

The Human Firewall Builder is storytelling using life experiences and characters that are in relatable situations, so you do not have to learn through your own horrible real-life mistakes, data breaches, malware outbreaks or identity theft events.

I also found that learning a topic such as cybersecurity can be challenging and that the subjects may seem overly technical and complicated. To alleviate some of the challenges I use scenarios that many of the readers will find relatable to their own daily lives, the lives of friends, family, co-workers and more.

I created seven characters for seven days of the week which we will follow for one week. We build your human firewall in seven days as we navigate the day to day experiences of our seven characters. The characters, events and circumstances are meant to teach while entertaining.

The storylines, steps and depth of the subject matter are purposely brief but detailed enough to educate, maintain your attention and inspire you to seek out more information to further build your human firewall.

Human Firewall Building is not a one-time exercise; it is a continuous effort that through regular practice will protect you and your crown jewels.

About the Author

Michael Marrano is more than a certified cybersecurity expert, witty educator and entertaining speaker; he is also a real-world technology and information security practitioner who has been honing his skills for the last three decades.

Michael is also a Certified Information Systems Security Professional (CISSP), Certified Information Security Manager (CISM), and Certified Information Systems Auditor (CISA) with experience in consulting and executive business leadership roles.

Husband, father, and brother are some of Michael's titles that radiate his protective nature. A lifelong New Yorker with a self-proclaimed balance of book, street, and common-sense smarts makes his presentations both educational and entertaining and his war stories relatable.

Today Michael provides high-touch technology and information security consulting services to corporate and personal clients, small business owners, financial institutions, and anywhere else the "crown jewels" need protecting.

Michael began developing his security skill set in the mid-1990s while working in physical security and studying Security and the Criminal Justice system at St. John's University.
Even during his college years, Michael was a proactive thinker and planner who had already performed the necessary steps to enter law enforcement after graduation.

It was priorities at home that caused a temporary halt to his law enforcement career pursuits and ultimately changed his career path forever.

Curiosity and a desire to know how stuff works attracted Michael to technology and ultimately a career that already spans three decades. As a self-taught technologist, Michael's career and skills have taken him to Fortune 500 companies, the most significant financial trading floors in the world and through the career ranks to executive level positions such as Managing Director, Chief Technology Officer (CTO) and Chief Information Security Officer (CISO).

Michael is dedicated to educating and creating awareness about technology and cybersecurity benefits and risks. While in the consulting sector, he recognized the need to empower people to be better prepared to confidently handle cybersecurity threats, create and manage strong information security programs, and understand ever-changing regulations at the corporate and personal level.

Michael is a Human firewall builder using his enhanced cybersecurity awareness and survivability programs to defend corporate and personal assets in the face of the ever-increasing threat of cyber-attacks.

Introduction to Human Firewall Building

Let me start with some good news, the good news is you have invested a few bucks into purchasing this book and with a little time and energy can begin transforming from the weakest link into a human firewall. The bad news is cybersecurity breaches make the news headlines seemingly daily.

Our private data is compromised at a greater frequency as Organizations, Governments, Businesses, and our Employers scramble to combat the threats and restructure their cyber defense tactics. Millions of Americans know too well the hardships of identity theft, data breaches, ransomware and countless other cybercrimes.

Your government has failed to protect your sensitive data, retailers have failed to protect your payment card data, social networks have failed to protect your privacy, the banks have been unable to protect your money, the healthcare system has been unable to protect your private medical data and your employers have failed to protect your workplace personally identifiable information.

It is easy to feel helpless in the endless battle against cybercriminals, hackers and scammers since so much of the attack surface is outside of your control. You cannot control how the government secures the social security system or how large corporations secure your payment card information but there are plenty of areas where you can strengthen your cybersecurity and that is what the human firewall builder is all about.

We cannot sit back relying on others and waiting for someone or something else to protect us from cyber harm. We cannot depend on a single security system or service for protection since there is no magic silver bullet software, hardware or service that is going to save us from the inevitable data breach. Corporations spend millions of dollars on security and technology, only to be hacked and breached by cyber-goons.

As individuals, small business owners, and non-techies we do not have the financial resources or the expertise to develop an enterprise strength security posture. There is no software upgrade or security patch for the gullible and untrained humans, but there is entertaining and educational material that can transform you from the weakest link into a human firewall.

Some more good news, human firewall building does not require investing millions or thousands and not even hundreds of dollars. Human Firewall building does not require technical skills or expensive computer equipment. Human firewall building does require time, persistence and commitment to a continuous effort of strengthening your defenses.

My definition of a "human firewall" is a proactive individual who is continuously preparing, always learning and building stronger defenses in the digital world and physical world. Human Firewalls know physical security is equally as important as technical cybersecurity.

The advice in this book is designed for all levels of technical knowledge and know-how. I wrote this book with my friends and family in mind and use these very same steps and advice to teach them how to protect themselves in the connected digital world of today. So, if you are wondering if this is the right book for you the answer is a big Hell Yeah!

History

Technology such as computers were initially designed to perform complex mathematical calculations and make difficult tasks easier for humans. The internet, email, smartphones, and internet connected devices (IoT) were also designed to make tasks easier for humans and to connect our communications.

Throughout the design, security has never been the highest priority and was an afterthought in a constant game of catch-up. To understand the current connected digital world, we first must take a quick look back at how we got here.

I promise not to bore you with a lengthy history of the internet since we all know the internet was invented by a former Vice President of ours. The internet of today was born in the early 1980s back when U2 concert tickets cost about $20 (compared to today's $300+) and the first publicized internet worm virus was released as a so-called academic project gone haywire in the late 80's.

The Morris worm aka Internet Worm exploited a few technical vulnerabilities that were later patched but the worm virus also exploited weak passwords. So, way back in 1988 missing software patches and weak passwords were security issues when there was estimated to be less than 100,000 computers connected to the internet. As of today (Fall 2018), there are estimated to be over 20 BILLION devices connected to the internet and guess what has not changed in 30+ years? Weak passwords and missing software patches are still security issues and being exploited. We are doomed if we continue to make the same mistakes and allow history to repeat itself.

Today the globally interconnected world has become a haven for criminals, rogue nations, organized crime and hacktivists, the technology we all cannot live without is regularly exploited due to the endless number of vulnerabilities in its original designs. Almost every week another security flaw, zero-day, malware that exploits an operating system, a vulnerability in a popular device and a security hole in a major corporation causes a breach.

End of the history lesson and the beginning of your Human Firewall building.

Day 1: Sunday

Introducing Betty B. aka "The Roaring Twenties"

Sunday #SundayFunday we meet Betty B., a twenty-something recent college grad working at her first professional job at a high-tech startup. For Betty the work week is filled with busy work days and evenings are for yoga, dog runs and the occasional happy hour.

Her weekends are spent relaxing, catching up with friends, family and household chores (laundry, cleaning, meal-prep) before preparing for the busy work week and all the other chaos that is typical of Mondays.

Smartphone security

Working at a tech firm Betty loves all things tech and she does not have the patience or willpower to wait for the lengthy approval process before new apps are approved and published to app stores.

She is using a jailbroken smartphone, so she can run an unpublished and unapproved version of a social messaging app developed by a new company that all her friends and colleagues are testing and use to communicate and locate each other. Betty is using her one and only personal smartphone to check the unpublished app and chat with other testers.

A few topics are covered in this scenario:
Mobile Security
Data Privacy
Mobile Apps
Jailbreaking

What should Betty be concerned about here?

The smartphones of today have more computing power than the first space shuttle to the moon and are essentially mini supercomputers. There are billions of smartphones in the world which makes for a desirable target for cybercriminals.

Smartphones were designed for communication and ease of use with security as an afterthought. Today smartphone manufacturers, and legit software developers consider privacy and security as a priority which is why apps go through a lengthy approval process and guidelines.

Developing your human firewall means securing your smartphone, your privacy, your communications and your life.

How can you build your human firewall and avoid making the same mistakes?

Here's how:

Step 1. Keep your device's operating system updated and all the apps updated as well. If you jailbreak the phone you are removing device restrictions that can leave your device vulnerable.

The device operating system may no longer receive updates and security patches and will no longer be supported by the manufacturer. You have essentially voided any warranty and technical support for the device.

Step 2. Only install apps from trusted sources. Regularly review the apps on your phone or tablet. Review the privacy settings and if you don't use an app anymore, delete it.

Deleting unused apps and keeping others current, including the operating system on your mobile devices will help reduce vulnerabilities on your smartphone.

Step 3. Physical security has and always will be an issue for smartphones and all small portable devices because smartphones cost as much as $1,000 or more.

They are a prime target for the local snatch and grab goons looking to make quick cash. Keep a vice-like grip on your device, store it out of sight and make sure the device is locked when not in use.

Step 4. Require the passcode or biometric to be entered or re-authenticate to access installed apps. This is a must do for apps such as email, banking, online shopping and others with access to sensitive data.

This will save your butt if someone steals your unlocked smartphone and will prevent the thief from getting into your installed apps and sensitive data.

Step 5. Lock your device with the longest allowed PIN or passcode. Even when a passcode or pin is optional. Going without a passcode lock is unthinkable when you consider the amount of personal information your phone contains. Most devices allow six characters so use a long, complex passcode.

Step 6. Find my Phone! Phones are expensive, contain lots of sensitive data and are easily misplaced, lost and stolen.

It seems like a no-brainer to take a few minutes to configure the lost device location services from your phone vendor.

Step 7. Keep it Private! Keep track of your phone operating system and app privacy settings and check the settings on a regular basis. The default settings will not keep you or your information safe.

Use the opt-out features for public view settings and information sharing. Limit app access to location services, address books, and personal photos.

Step 8. Check the privacy settings after updates and upgrades. Be sure to review new features after updates and app upgrades are installed because the new default settings of new features may create new privacy and security threats.

Privacy settings are being updated more often with the state, government and international privacy law changes, so it is critical to update your settings regularly.

Step 9. BYOD isn't for me! Don't use your personal devices for work. Keep work data and software off your personal laptop and smartphone. Many organizations can remotely wipe devices and manage the configuration including software.

They also may track the location of your smartphone which can become an issue if you're at a baseball game on your sick day. Ask your company to provide a work laptop and smartphone.

Step 10. Crash test dummy! Use a dummy smartphone, computer, virtual computer or sandbox for testing new software, apps and devices.

Do not use your primary device or computer to try new software, check a new program or connect untrusted devices. You want to keep your primary or only device secure if there is a blowup or vulnerability.

Social Media security

Betty B. uses her social media accounts as a personal blog to share her photos, life reflections and foodie reviews with her growing number of followers. Her Sunday morning starts off with a quick selfie of herself and her cute rescue pug Sammy lying in bed #Sundaze #Puglife #Bedhead.

The photo is quickly uploaded and shared across the usual suspects of social media for friends, family and strangers to like, comment and creep on.

A few topics are covered in this scenario:
Friend Requests
Untagging
Location Data
Digital Footprint

What should Betty be concerned about here?
Social media sites have connected us all and grown rapidly over the years, but we've paid the price for our connections.

The loss of individual privacy caused by the endless sharing of information has caused many of us to inadvertently expose ourselves in ways that can compromise our own safety and security. Along with your photos on the social networks, the digital footprints, and the personal information you leave behind can be hazardous regarding identity theft, stalking and other malicious ways.

The best way to protect yourself is to not make yourself vulnerable in the first place. Sharing our special moments (like the time you ate a whole pizza) on social networks allows us to stay connected with our friends and family but also opens our lives to strangers with potential malicious intentions. Abusing some of the information on social media profiles, criminals may be able to apply for credit cards, medical insurance, file income tax returns, open a bank account, or even register for a driver's license under your name.

How can you build your human firewall and avoid making the same mistakes?

Here's how:

Step 1. Don't overshare yourself! Look through your social media accounts as a hacker might and think of all the malicious ways you (a hacker) can exploit your full name, home address, pets names, email address, birthdate, and phone number.

All the postings, tags and pictures of your friends, family, coworkers, business affiliates and so much more can be used to steal identities, launch attacks on connections and invade your privacy. Remember nothing is genuinely private so be very careful what you post and share on social networks.

Step 2. Think before you Like! Whenever you engage in social networking, remember what happens on the internet stays on the internet, and it's up to you to make sure what appears in connection with your name, brand and image do not have the potential to harm you now or in the future.

This is especially true for young people who post without concern of what impact a posting will have when they apply for college, a job or meet the future love of their life.

Step 3. You have enough friends! Seriously, how many friends do you really need anyway plus a true friend is someone you can call when you need to move a couch (how to get friends to help you move a couch book is coming soon).

Only accept invitations to connect online with people you know well in real life and unfriend people you do not know in the real world. Be aware of the fact that bad guys will use you to get close to your friends and affiliates.

Step 4. Bad guys know you can't go two minutes without liking a food picture or sending a DM to your friends on social networks.

Since social networking can increase your data charges, be very careful when trying to save a few bucks and data bits by connecting to public and untrusted Wi-Fi networks which can leave you vulnerable to hackers, who could then use the Internet connection to glean all kinds of private information from your laptop, tablet, or phone. Avoid public and unprotected wireless networks and use a VPN to reduce the risk.

Step 5. Limit your public broadcasts! Think twice before making announcements that could be used to exploit your vulnerability such as announcing you are away on vacation and your home may be empty and unprotected.

TMI (too much information) seems like a no-brainer to take a moment before you share your announcements on social networks since once your information is posted publicly, you have little control over who may view it and exploit the information.

Step 6. Untag yourself from all those social network pictures of your friends playing beer pong or performing keg stands when you called out sick from work.

Each site has different instructions and many offer mass untagging so start cleaning that "good stuff" up now before your boss or grandma finds out what you have been doing.

Step 7. Develop a new "wholesome" Digital Footprint by creating a blog on volunteering, post your favorite cooking recipes, start commenting on reputable news sites and begin adding legitimate reviews for online purchases (not your shady dark web dealings).

This step will help create a new page one on the popular search engines and push all the other stuff to the back pages.

Wireless Network security

Betty recently moved into her apartment in the city and is still waiting for her cable and internet connection to be installed but no worries since she lives in an apartment building and there are more than a dozen wireless networks in range.

She also lives on the third floor and can also connect to the city wireless network "CityLink" from a nearby kiosk access point. During a wireless network scan, she found an open wireless network that did not require a password.

Score, free internet and maybe she can cancel that new internet connection install and save a few bucks!

A few topics are covered in this scenario:
Open Networks
Personal VPN
HTTPS "Yellow Padlock"
Firewalls

What should Betty be concerned about here?

We all find ourselves in this same situation on a regular basis either at home, traveling, or in our own neighborhood. We are surrounded by open, guest, and free wireless networks and since mobile internet data charges are expensive, we are all tempted to connect to an untrusted network.

A trip to the local coffee shop, the gym, your doctor's office, and even the town or city you live in is also broadcasting free wireless internet. There is a cost that comes with connecting to an untrusted network and it may be more than you ever expected to pay if your identity is stolen.

If you must connect to untrusted networks for whatever crazy reasoning, you have to make sure you have security software (antivirus) installed, the latest operating systems updates, software patches, strong passwords and a personal VPN.

How can you build your human firewall and avoid making the same mistakes?

Here's how:

Step 1. Do not trust untrusted networks! If you must connect to an untrusted, open, guest or any network you cannot trust then you must limit your activity.

Paying your bills, performing your holiday shopping, downloading medical records or anything else that might be highly sensitive should only be done on a computer and network you can trust.

Check movie times or look up a restaurant but do not use your credit cards when connected to an open network.

Step 2. Autopilot for Updates! You need to perform regular updates no matter which operating system you use. Microsoft Windows operating systems are updated monthly, typically on so-called Patch Tuesday.

Apple and Android operating systems are also updated frequently on a regular schedule. You should set your operating system to update automatically when new updates become available.

Step 3. Upgrade web browsers! No matter which browser you use, it is super important that you update it as newer versions come out to address security threats and vulnerabilities.

Most browsers will automatically deliver updates on a frequent schedule every few weeks but do not just set it and forget it.

Step 4. Let's get personal about VPNs. Personal VPN software on your computer, phone and laptop will help protect your privacy and secure your traffic as you use the internet.

A personal VPN is a must have when traveling and connected to untrusted networks. Purchase a personal VPN from a reputable software vendor and avoid the freebies.

Step 5. Resist the urge to reuse passwords across different sites and services. This also goes for the websites you consider bullshit sites (any site with your email, full name, credit card or address is not a BS site) cause you think no one will ever target your cooking recipe websites or your do-it-yourself home and garden blogs.

Those BS websites have the lowest security budgets and your info is good as gone the first time a cybercriminal sets sights on the website.

Step 6. Change your passwords even if you don't have too! It's true that many sites and services will never force you to change your password and it's also true that no one will force you to change your underwear, but I hope you still change both on a frequent basis.

Add a calendar reminder for a day or two that are your password changing dates to voluntarily change your passwords across all your sites and services.

Step 7. Antivirus software that's either free or for-fee is much better than nothing. There is no excuse for not having antivirus software installed on your computers.

It is true that modern malware and viruses can evade antivirus software, but there are way more types and versions of malicious software that will be stopped by a current and regularly updated virus definition library.

Step 8. Two steps are better than one! Practically every email service from Microsoft's Outlook to Gmail, Yahoo Mail and Hotmail has a feature called "Multi-Factor Authentication" or MFA or "Two Step Verification" or 2FA. It requires an additional verification step to gain access to the email account.

After a user's signs-in with ID and password, they are prompted to enter a secret pin code. To prevent unauthorized access to your email, you must activate MFA!

Step 9. Look for the Lock! Look for the padlock symbol on the address bar before submitting any private information.

Do verify that sites use TLS (Transport Layer Security) encryption. People still call the lock SSL, but that is an old encryption that is no longer secure.

Make sure the URL begins with "HTTPS," not just "HTTP." The S is for Secure and newer web browsers will warn you when the website is not secured.

Step 10. Layer up like it's a cold winter day! The defense in depth method is an old military term that also works very well in building our human firewall.

Using multiple security tools such as dedicated anti-malware alongside your traditional anti-virus solutions. Put up a fence, big a moat, release the hounds and anything else that will slow down an attacker.

Step 11. If your network hardware is included in your service and provided by your cable, phone or internet service provider don't automatically assume your security is in good hands and worry free.

As I sit here writing this book I see several wireless networks broadcasting the name of the service provider in the SSID.

If you have had the same service provider and hardware for a few years, you may also be due for an upgrade which you should initiate by requesting a hardware upgrade to get the latest security features and services. Don't wait!

Step 12. Sharing is caring! Wait, you didn't know you were sharing your bandwidth with your service providers other customers.

If your service provider is offering nationwide Wi-Fi access to thousands or more wireless hotspots, it's because all customers are configured by default to broadcast the public wireless network. That means random people passing by your home could use the hotspot to get on the Internet.

If you don't want to be part of the public hotspot network or hidden network, you must opt out of the service by updating your account settings online or calling customer service.
☐

Digital Assistant security

Our girl Betty is always looking for ways to get more stuff done with less time and these days who isn't. She leverages her virtual digital assistants to accomplish her daily goals and make life easier.

She depends on Alexa, Cortana, Siri and more to order groceries, schedule appointments, read emails, play music and receive news and weather alerts.

Her VDA's even help track her health and workouts which is fantastic because she is in a competition with her friends to see who can walk the most steps and burn the most calories each day.

Betty is crushing her fitness goals today because she and her wearable fitness tracker are heading to the gym, errands and a shop till you drop shopping spree.

A few topics are covered in this scenario:
Wearable Devices
Digital Assistants
Location Tracking
Smart Devices

What should Betty be concerned about in this scenario?

Over the past few years the rise of the machines aka virtual digital assistants (VDAs) has flourished with the adoption of Apple Siri, Microsoft Cortana, Amazon's Alexa and Googles Home into our homes to help us order food, control lighting, manage temperature, play our favorite love songs, lock our doors and much more.

We have even seen Amazon Echo also known as Alexa recordings used as evidence in a murder case which brings up a high point of concern which is these devices are always listening. A VDA works by always listening for the "wake up word" – "Siri" "OK Google" "Cortana" "Alexa" or "Amazon," and then records your voice and transfers it to a processor for analysis so that it can fulfill requests or answer questions.

The recordings are streamed and stored remotely and can be reviewed or deleted over time which rolls into my next point which is the data is stored on the vendor's servers and what we have learned from the many data breaches is vendors get hacked all the time.

How can you build your human firewall and avoid making the same mistakes?

Here's how:

Step 1. Treat your VDA's like all other IoT (Smart) devices and perform regular software updates and patches.

Enable auto-update features but also check the version on a regular basis. Don't just set it and forget it, conduct periodic reviews for missing updates.
Step 2. Consider a separate network for your VDA's and IoT devices, so the devices are not "mingling" with your personal computer and sensitive data.

Smart devices do not have the same security features and if the "smart" device network is compromised the digital assistant settings can be changed, or the device reset and used to exploit and attack other devices on the network.

Step 3. Zip it! Turn off voice purchasing or add a pin code to keep your prankster friends from yelling out "hey Alexa order me a pizza and garlic breadsticks". Seriously, at least add some pepperoni or sausage to the pizza.

A nearby television, radio or person speaking on the phone can trigger an unintentional purchase or something more malicious and less delicious.

Step 4. Drop the mic! Turn off VDA microphones and cameras when not in use to prevent a hacked device from being used to eavesdrop or spy.

Also, the always listening microphone can potentially malfunction from noise from the radio, TV, computer or even other digital assistants.

Step 5. You will cry the blues when you get bluejacked! There are new Bluetooth exploits all the time and we won't get into the long list of threats or technical details except for that if you are using Bluetooth while out in the world you are potentially exposing yourself to a host of unwanted exploits and unauthorized access to your devices.

Keep your devices patched and updated with the latest software version and disable Bluetooth when it's not in use.

Step 6. Wear and tear! Wearable technology is becoming more popular every day but like many other new technologies' security has been an afterthought and speed to market has been a priority.

Often, we think of wearable technology as a smartwatch or fitness monitor, but medical devices such as pacemakers, artificial hearts, insulin pumps and other bionic implants can be compromised.

A hacker can access personal information, location data or potentially kill someone with a lethal dose or deactivate a wearable medical device. Be sure you research the threats to your wearable devices and understand what is at risk.

Step 7. I have the POWER (try shouting that in your best He-Man voice). Cybercriminals love to use the power of billions of smart devices like our digital assistants for large-scale attacks and other mayhem.

Many of these devices have little or no built-in security which leaves them vulnerable to exploit. Research each of your devices for known security bugs, disable any unnecessary features (like remote management) and use unique credentials for each device.

Step 8. Out with the old and in with the new! Pay attention to the lifecycle of smart devices, wearable tech, and digital assistants.

Check the manufacturers website for firmware software updates and when a sunset (retirement) is announced you need to plan your replacement. If the manufacturer is no longer supporting the device or is out of business, you should immediately find a replacement.

Photo Sharing security

Betty loves taking pictures and videos to share with friends, family and her legions of followers on various social networks.

She started out taking pictures during her travels and what started out as a hobby has become a side hustle that's starting to earn a nice chunk of change. She has begun to sell her photos and has also been hired to take pictures at events.

For picture storage and sharing with clients, she is using a cloud service that provides her enough space for free to get the job and clients seem to enjoy the easy access.

A few topics are covered in this scenario:
Privacy
Cloud Services
Free Services
IP (Intellectual Property)

What should Betty be concerned about in this scenario?

Practically all traces of your online activity are captured, archived and used to develop a profile or "digital footprint". The same is true about pictures we take, post on social networks, upload to photo sharing websites.

Everything about the photo including the location, people tagged in the photo and items in the picture are recorded and tracked by data miners and information harvesters.

Digital footprint data is useful to marketers and the reason why sneaker ads seem to follow you everywhere and on all devices after shopping online for a new pair of kicks.

Digital footprints can also be traced by employers, schools, creditors and attract the attention of cybercriminals out to steal your identity or online creeps and pervs looking for a new obsession to stalk.

How can you build your human firewall and avoid making the same mistakes?

Here's how:

Step 1. Social networks and photo share sites are not a family photo album. Consider whether your picture is appropriate or whether it could cause embarrassment or future harm to your family members.

This is also very true when posting pictures of your kids and someone else's kids. Imagine if a fun picture of your adorable grandma turns into the latest viral meme.

Step 2. Once is not enough! Check the privacy settings not just once but regularly, to ensure that they haven't changed because they are always changing.

Also review the rules, regulations and photo ownership, so you know what happens to the pictures if you delete your account. You want to make sure the images are deleted if you deactivate your account.

Step 3. Hide and Seek! GPS-enabled phones, geotags, and location tracking integrated into photos may leak private information such as where you live and places you spend time.

You may unknowingly offer up sensitive information like your work address, your home address, and other places you frequent. This information can easily be abused by a cybercriminal, creepy stalker or internet troll.

Step 4. No do-overs! Once you've posted or shared a picture, that's it, there's no way to take it back. It's always out there, on a server, someone else's computer, or printed somewhere.

Even if you tighten up your privacy settings, a picture shared online will become public property and out of your control.

If you share an image then quickly delete it, there is no telling that someone had not saved it to their computer or reposted somewhere else.

Step 5. Your pictures are out of control! Seriously once you share or post a picture anyone copy, tag, save, reuse, and lots more without your consent.

When you signed up for your social network and photo sharing site access, you quickly clicked through the "terms and conditions" which typically gives your permission to release ownership of any media you share.

You basically approved the use of the photo and video in any way the site owner deems fit for use. One way to avoid this fiasco is to only use paid subscription platforms and encrypt the data with your own encryption key.

Step 6. Primetime and billboards! It would be awesome if your photo landed on a billboard advertisement or a network television commercial. It would be awesome if you were getting paid for the picture.

Online photos and videos are often grabbed and used by commercial entities without consent and without compensation. If you want to make money with your photos add your own watermark.

Step 7. Never-neverland! Never ever geotag photos containing kids. It does not matter if they are your kids or someone else's children.

You are potentially letting creeps, stalkers, and the worst of society know where to find those children. Also, never geotag your home for the same reasons.

Sunday Takeaways:

Technology is embedded in our lives to a point where every waking moment is spent in front of a screen. There are now generations who have grown from children to adults with technology along the entire way.

The love affair with technology started as childhood learning tools, to social network communication during school years and into their professional lives. Using smartphone apps to connect to social media and photo sharing on public networks or utilizing a digital assistant to reduce your personal and professional workload are just a few of the perks of modern technology.

It is imperative that you never underestimate the threats lurking in your daily digital life. The threats are not as obvious as a masked robber or shady character on the street corner.

Human firewalls still practice the childhood term "stranger danger" which still applies in your digital life so limit your exposure, public sharing and talking to strangers.

Day 2: Monday

Introducing: Pauly B. aka "The Family Guy"

Mondays can be manic #manicmonday. Today we follow a man with a plan who also plays in a rock n roll band. Mondays are hectic after a busy weekend of playing gigs with the band.

Our man with a plan is Pauly B, who has a few job titles of which the most important is his gig as full-time dad and family man. Pauly is the go-to resource for everything at home including technical and financial support.

Home Network security

Our pal Pauly is also Mr. Fix it at home, so when his family members complain about slow internet, he jumps into action. He is going for father of the year award by upgrading his family internet bandwidth speed to support the latest video streaming and online gaming systems.

The local cable company is charging $20 bucks per month for cable router rental, so Pauly opts to purchase his own preowned router at a bargain price from an online auction site to save some dough for his family.

A few topics are covered in this scenario:
Supply Chain
Used Technology
Firmware Updates
Wireless Security

What should Pauly be concerned about in this scenario?

Without getting into statistics and quoting sources it's safe to say that nearly every home in America has at least one personal computer and in many homes, there are at least one computer, smart device and mobile device per family member.

How many of those homes and families have an IT Professional or a Chief Information Security Officer (CISO) managing the home network and computers?

I'm willing to bet a few bitcoins that most homes are unprepared and poorly staffed in the IT/IS Department and since many homes contain as much technology as a small business, they are a prime target for cybercriminals.

How can you build your human firewall and avoid making the same mistakes?

Here's how:

Step 1. Born to be a techie! You're a self-taught techie wizard Rockstar; you manage the networks and hardware for your own home, friends and family so please change the default password and make sure the new passwords are very long and complicated phrases.

The super-user passwords should be unique and not in use anywhere else. Also, avoid the temptation of writing the password on the device.

Step 2. Technology becomes outdated faster than ice cream melts on a hot day. Preowned, used, secondhand tech can potentially contain malware, spyware, rootkit backdoors and other malicious software.

If you must use previously used tech be sure to perform a factory reset on the device, update the firmware and change the default password asap.

Step 3. Smithsonian! Do not be a historian of old operating systems (OS) or old tech devices. If you use obsolete devices, software or OS's you will no longer receive software updates from the manufacturer, including security updates that can help protect your devices from harmful viruses and malware.

Step 4. No fault! A breach is all your fault if you still use the default! Change the default name of your wireless network, so you're not broadcasting the make and model of the device.

Also stop giving away your service provider name, identity and location with your SSID. Using the internet service provider's name, your own name or apartment number in your wireless network name is just asking for trouble.

Use something less obvious or even potentially dangerous to connect to like "Virus Test Lab Wireless" to keep potential intruders away. Think of it as a fake "beware of dog" sign.

Step 5. Skies not the limits! Know your limitations and If securing your home network seems to be a stretch of your technical skills you should tap out. Contact a professional or friend who happens to be an IT Professional for help.

A small investment in configuring and securing your home network will pay off dearly in the long run. I have earned many beers and pizzas over the years helping friends and family secure their systems, home and small business networks #willworkforfood.

Step 6. Timeout! Limit your family members and children's ability to add devices to your network and protect access to network hardware accounts with administrative privileges.

This will help prevent unknown and potential unsecured software and devices from connecting to your network.

Also consider adding restrictions to limit the amount of time family members can spend online or on social networks.

Step 7. Use a router or security appliance device with advanced security features such as network access control, web filtering, intrusion protection, automatic updates and anything else available that keeps family members from clicking on the malicious links, visiting the wrong sites and keeps rogue devices off your network.

Mobile Device security

As a parent, you are the human firewall for your family and children and Pauly's family is always on the go and so is their technology.

The family all have laptops, smartphones, smartwatches and tablets for school, work and personal use. Mr. B is charged with supporting and maintaining all the devices and is a self-proclaimed family technical guru.

Occasionally there is a meltdown that requires a device to sit on the sidelines for repairs but there are enough devices to go around and sharing is never a problem.

A few topics are covered in this scenario:
Data Backup
Device Inventory
Antivirus
Device Sharing

What should Pauly be concerned about in this scenario?

These days your devices are always on the move. Your home and business networks may very well be hardened fortresses, but when you are out in the world traveling with your technology, it is even more essential to practice human firewall behavior.

The more we travel and access the Internet on the go, the more threats we face. No one is safe from the threat of cybercriminals when outside their trusted home and work networks.

Family members sharing devices seems harmless, but kids are just as likely to click links, open attachments and connect to the untrusted network as adults.

How can you build your human firewall and avoid making the same mistakes?

Here's how:

Step 1. Don't share your computer! Use a separate computer for all your grownup stuff such as paying bills, managing finances, your job!

One of the safest measures you can take to protect yourself (and family) is to use an adult-only designated computer. Kids are more likely to install software, click on malicious links, and download email attachments that may give cybercriminals access to your computer and information using programs.

Step 2. Smartphones don't float! With all the features and technology breakthroughs you would think that someone could make a smartphone that floats.

Until that happens, make sure you have a backup of your important contacts, documents and family pictures. This will help you avoid the devastating loss of all your photos when you drop your phone in a toilet.

Step 3. SIM Swappers and SIM Jackers! It is scary how easy hackers can social engineer mobile provider customer support into authorizing a SIM swap.

A SIM card is used by the providers to identify your mobile device on the network, so the mobile provider can send calls and data to your device. A hacker can convince your mobile provider to route those calls and messages to other devices, so they can intercept emails, security codes, password resets and more.

To help reduce the threat, mobile providers allow an extra security pin to be added to the account, but it's not required, and you must set it up. Set up the security pin code asap and make sure it's a unique code.

Step 4. Join the chain gang! Invest in a security chain for your mobile devices and use them while in public places or anywhere else you can anchor your laptop to a heavy object.

Make the local snatch and grab goons work hard if they want to steal your laptop.

Step 5. Give shoulder surfers eye strain! Purchase privacy screens for all your devices. A privacy screen makes it very difficult to view what is on your screen if you are not directly in front of the screen.

Shoulder surfers, the curious and just plain nosey people are everywhere and snooping. In many cases it is easier to shoulder surf while you are entering your credentials to gain access than trying to hack your account.

Step 6. Idle time is a vulnerable time. Set your devices to automatically lock when idle for a short period of time.

I strongly suggest a one-minute idle time lock on all mobile devices because a lot can happen in a New York minute. Just imagine a mobile device left behind in a taxi or subway!

Step 7. Sharing is caring but don't share your passwords with anyone (even family members). I know this is going to cause a few waves in some households when spouses stop sharing passwords and credentials but before you contact a divorce attorney.

If there is no way to avoid the sharing at least use the secure sharing function in a password manager or vault.

Step 8. Super kids are fantastic but kids with superuser access is a recipe for disaster. Ensure that system administrators and superusers accounts are protected.

Most family members only need a basic everyday non-administrative account for reading email, accessing the Internet, and composing documents.

Step 9. Whitelist list the good and blacklist the bad. If you're a Parent (or a business owner), you must develop a family policy for managing and preventing downloading and installing software to your network and devices.

Preventing the install and use of non-approved applications via application whitelisting will make your devices more secure and prevent unauthorized and unsupported software installs.

Step 10. Treat someone else's web browser like someone else's toothbrush and don't use it! Browsers can be configured to automatically save sensitive data such as credit cards, passwords and form data.

Activities such as banking or shopping should only be done on a device that belongs to you, on a device that you trust. Whether it's a relative's device, a friend's computer, or a public kiosk computer you can expect your sensitive data to be copied, stolen and exploited.

Step 11. Have at least one backup copy of data offline or disconnected from your computer network. This is an essential part of your backup strategy to recover from ransomware attacks.

Ransomware variants will target backup jobs and having an offline copy will help avoid a ransomware attack from hijacking all your valuable data.

Step 12. Don't put off backing up your important data and don't rely on your lousy memory to remind you to perform your next backup job.

Automate weekly or even better a daily backup on all computers and devices that contain important information.

Also, make sure your backups are encrypted to protect the data from prying eyes or the inevitable data breach of your backup service provider.

Step 13. Get basic! Antivirus is one of the most basic protections and we all must focus on the basics when developing our human firewall. Antivirus software is inexpensive and can even easily be found for free.

Using free or for-fee software will help prevent virus and malicious software from causing damage. There is no excuse for not using antivirus.

Step 14. Autopilot! Configure auto-update for the software and firmware on your network gear and hardware on a regular basis.

Many devices can be configured for auto-update, but you still should periodically check to make sure the updates are working.

Avoid the set it and forget it mentality by performing regular update inspections to check that auto updates are running and backup the configurations of the devices.

Step 15. Bingo! You won't be yelling Bingo when you get a virus. Malware and viruses may also creep into popular online and app gaming.

Criminals will often create counterfeit versions of popular games and offer the games on third-party websites and fake app stores for free or less than the price of the original game.

Scammers may advertise a "new release" or "new feature pack" to reel in a new catch. Game malware is a growing concern and must be guarded against as you crush candy.

Internet-of-Things security

Pauly is a one-man army at home, but even a domestic warrior such as Paul knows he has limitations and must delegate some of his workloads.

He is using smart devices to assist with managing his household and chores. The family's smart thermostat will regulate the temperature in the home and send updates to Paul on ways to reduce energy consumption.

The smart refrigerator will keep track of the family grocery shopping list, no more dry grass or bushes since the smart sprinkler system will maintain the landscape watering schedule and even the car emails him oil change reminders.

Paul can just sit back and drink beers on his patio now that he is living the life of the futuristic Jetsons family.

A few topics are covered in this scenario:
Smart Devices
Network Security
Default Credentials

Remote Access

What should Pauly be concerned about in this scenario?

The tremendous growth and benefits of internet-connected devices, systems and services collectively known as the Internet-of-Things (IoT) is undeniable.

The harsh reality is security is not keeping up with the growth and sadly in many cases security was not even planned in the development of the devices.

The fact that product designers, developers and manufacturers take shortcuts to get products to market quickly is nothing new and is just another supporting reason why we all need to be proactive about building our own human firewall.

Security is an afterthought in many of the smart devices and systems we all use each day. The lack of security functions and features compounded by poor cyber-hygiene has created countless vulnerabilities that cannot be easily patched.

There have been and will be more armies of vulnerable Botnet IoT devices set to cause mayhem such as distributed denial of service (DDoS) on businesses, governments, websites and internet service providers.

Your own self-aware, neglected and jealous home thermostat or smart TV may be launching its own attack on your latest new gadget causing an all IoT war in your home.

That last sentence is only my personal prediction and not supported by any current evidence but with all the A.I. (artificial intelligence) developments, I bet this happens very soon.

How can you build your human firewall and avoid making the same mistakes?

Here's how:

Step 1. Life is short and so is the security of default passwords! Change the default passwords on the devices as soon as possible.

The default passwords for popular devices can easily be found doing a quick online search. Make sure to use a long and complex password phrase. Don't write the password on the device!

Step 2. Install software updates, firmware and patches on the IoT devices on a regular basis. If available, set the device to auto-update.

If the devices are no longer supported by the manufacturer, it should be replaced with a newer modern device.

Step 3. Register the devices with the manufacturer to subscribe to news, security warnings and end of life alerts.

An older IoT device may work great but past its End of Life (EOL) which means it's no longer supported or receives software and security updates which will make it an easy target for hackers to exploit.

Step 4. Most home networking routers allow separation of devices to create an IoT network with restrictions to the internet.

Limiting access in and out will reduce the external threats to the devices and the threat from other devices inside your home.

Step 5. Dumb things down! You don't have to connect every smart device and you can always turn off unused devices.

Save a few bucks when purchasing appliances and go for an old-fashioned unconnected "dumb" refrigerator because you are smart enough to remember your grocery shopping list of beer, beer and more beer.

Step 6. Take an inventory of all your IoT devices. Go a step further and also list the dependencies of each IoT and deactivate any unnecessary services. Universal Plug and Play (UPnP) is a perfect example of a service that does more harm than good and should be turned off.

Remove old devices from your network such as that old baby monitor uploading data to the cloud and that potato chip Dash button ordering chips when the supply is low.

Step 7. Don't get played! Video game consoles have become supercomputer multimedia entertainment systems. The gaming consoles require frequent software updates and security patches like any other computer system.

Some also include motion detection cameras and microphones which are activated out of the box and can be exploited by an attacker if they are not secured or deactivated. Keep your gaming systems updated, behind a firewall and disable unnecessary features.

Family Jewels security

Pauly is a jack of all trades as the family accountant, finance pro and one-man incident response team. He is also a tree lover and has chosen to go paperless for all the family financial statements, bills and invoices.

Pauly also uses an online accounting platform to keep track of expenses and another service to monitor for unauthorized financial activity and identity protection.

In addition to saving for a rainy day, he is planning to keep his family safe and dry on rainy days or more significant events including natural disasters and cyber incidents.

A few topics are covered in this scenario:
Financial Monitoring
Separation of Duties
Phishy Emails
Disaster Plan

What should Pauly be concerned about in this scenario?

A parent has many hats to wear including protectors of the family financial assets and identities. The family jewels can be the obvious cash, credit card numbers, debit cards, gift cards, cryptocurrency, identification, social security number, tax ID, passport, drivers licenses ID, medical insurance BUT also the less obvious financial statements, tax returns, wills, deeds, birth certificates, jewelry, coin collection, works of art, rare stamps, old baseball cards, and comic book collectibles.

Parents need to consider adults aren't the only targets for identity theft. Criminals target the social security numbers of children because they are less likely to be monitored and protected.

Many parents may not think to check their child's credit history or request an annual report. Criminals may get away with stealing a child's identity for years because kids won't typically access their credit history until they start applying for school loans or credit cards.

How can you build your human firewall and avoid making the same mistakes?

Here's how:

Step 1. Family Jewels! Know what you need to protect. What are your "crown jewels"? Your most valuable assets may be your finances (money, investments, credit), reputation, affiliations and your identity. Understanding what your assets are will help you focus on threat protection.

Step 2. Separation of duties! Use different email addresses for different account types and for important services.

This step may catch that phishing email claiming to be from your boss when it comes to the account you use only for family communication, you know it's bogus.

Setting up an alternate email address to separate sections (work, personal, family, finances, etc.) of your life and communications will help reduce the threat lurking in spam and phishing emails.

Step 3. Teach your kids! Teach kids how valuable their identity is to cybercriminals and why they need to be very cautious with their personal information.

To help protect their child's identity, parents should request their child's credit report each year.

Step 4. If your children have their own online accounts and services, check their privacy settings. The default settings may expose more information than you'd like.

Change settings to the highest level of privacy. You never know who is snooping around their social media profiles. Teach your kids not to accept friend requests from people they don't know.

Step 5. Google yourself and family members! Don't stop with Google, Bing yourself and even give yourself a Yahoo-ing.

In other words, use the popular search engines to search your family member names, nicknames, email addresses and review the first few pages of results.

It is very important if you have a common name you may have to add more details like city and state but keep trying until you get to the good stuff.

If any of the "good stuff" is actually bad stuff you should contact the website to remove the information.

Step 6. Go paperless! One less bank statement, credit card bill and tax document for the dumpster divers and your shredder.

Almost all financial services and banks offer paperless statements these days, but you must request paperless so go through your account settings and opt-in for paperless.

Step 7. Stop giving away your personal information. Make the bad guys work hard for your personal information, so hard that they give up and move along to an easier target who didn't read this book.

Stop giving away your birthday on social media, your family history on ancestry websites, your place of work on job boards and resume sites and please stop sharing your location with everyone.

Step 8. The most significant investment of your life may also be a cyber criminals biggest score. Real estate is super expensive these days, and the demand is high which means things move fast with rapid transactions for all involved parties.

The many parties involved, the high number of emails exchanged during a deal is countless with numerous documents changing hands, digital e-signatures passing to different entities, and more is overwhelming, and this is where the cybercriminals find opportunity. Use out of band communications to verify transaction details before sending any money.

Step 9. Plan ahead, or you may end up dead! Develop a family emergency communication plan that includes a hard copy of household contact information because no one memorizes phone numbers anymore and without a mobile phone or electronic address it will be difficult to communicate.

Include contact information for family members, relatives, schools, workplaces, local police, fire department, doctors and nearby hospitals.

Step 10. Meet up! Decide right now where your family is going to meet if there is a disaster while everyone is separated.

Pick a couple of safe and accessible locations where the family can reunite. Consider a place that is capable of withstanding weather events or other disasters.

Also, consider a meeting location within your neighborhood and another out of town and further away if you must get away from your hometown.

Step 11. Band of brothers! Adults and children are playing more games online that have become social chat rooms. Some of the games create groups of random strangers to team up and play together and allow conversation during the game.

This can be particularly dangerous when the gaming groups are made up of adults and children. Educate your kids to the dangers and review your kid's gaming profiles to confirm they are age appropriate and they are not making any new "friends" in the online gaming world.

Tech Disposal security

Pauly and his family are always buying the latest and greatest technology and devices so as older devices are retired by the family. Pauly is charged with disposal of the old "tech junk".

He likes to take advantage of trade-in offers for discounts on new devices, sells (repurposes) lightly used devices online and takes advantage of free local technology recycling programs rather than just tossing the hardware into a landfill.

A few topics are covered in this scenario:
Data Disposal
Hardware Disposal
Hardware Inventory
Certificate of Destruction

What should Pauly be concerned about in this scenario?

The need for good security practices doesn't go away just because a system has outlived its usefulness.

Disposal of old technology and information must be performed in a way that you don't throw out your sensitive data and "crown jewels" with your old tech junk.

The same is true for old accounts and services which may contain sensitive data after you move on to another service provider.

Having a data and device disposal plan will help ensure that decommissioned equipment, accounts and services do not pose a threat.

How can you build your human firewall and avoid making the same mistakes?

Here's how:

Step 1. Take stock! Know what technology you have in your house, business and family! Keep a full and up-to-date inventory of your family and home technology devices including what each device is doing, when it was purchased and how critical it is to the overall home and family infrastructure.

Use a network or wireless router monitoring feature to alert you of new connected devices and maintain a network inventory of devices.

Step 2. Knowing is half the battle! Know where your valuable assets live. Does your hard-earned cash sit in a bank or in your mattress?

How about all your important files, are they on your laptop hard drive or in the cloud?

Do you manage your assets or do others have access? Knowing where the important stuff lives will keep you from accidentally throwing out your cash in the old mattress and your saved password and credit card data on an old hard drive.

Step 3. Your Digi-Doggy is long gone! Your online pets starved to death almost a decade ago, you will never attend a virtual high school class reunion and that food delivery services do not even deliver to your new home in the burbs, but your login credentials, credit card info and profile are still alive and kicking.

The truth is we all are guilty of signing up, registering and providing sensitive information that we leave behind when we move on to the next shiny new fad and service. Go back to clean up and delete your old accounts before they are breached by cyber-crooks.

Step 4. Take out the trash! Your trash is a dumpster divers' treasure! Don't assume that tossing old hard drives, network hardware, and obsolete tech gadgets into recycling, trash or landfill is secure.

If there's sensitive data, such as old passwords or even your home wireless credentials you need to erase, format, physically destroy it before throwing it away.

Step 5. Encrypt to give criminals the slip. Even reformatting or factory reset a device to "erase" the data it stores isn't good enough these days.

Encrypting the data on the drive before doing any deletion can help make data even more difficult to recover later but physically destroying the old drives and equipment is the best way to ensure it is truly trashed.

Step 6. Get in the know! Know what software is installed on your systems, what vendors have your information and what services you are paying for.

Create an inventory of the software and services you depend on but also the other random apps that count your footsteps, track your macros and remind you to call your mom on her birthday.

Note the location as on-premises or in the cloud, so you know where the data lives. Include license and subscription information especially the ones that have your credit card information and are set to auto renewal.

Monday Takeaways:

Our families, friends, co-workers and everyone else out there is connected by technology and the internet. The physical walls of our buildings and homes are not capable of keeping the digital intruders at bay and our most precious assets are no longer in our own possession.

Technology can be complicated, and the truth is most people do not have the resources or skills to secure their systems and services adequately. It's important to understand the basics, your own limitations and where to go for help.

New technology and services must be configured to be secure since off the shelf, out of the box, and default configurations leave gaping security and privacy holes.

As technology devices and services age, they must be maintained and updated on a recurring basis. A set it and forget it mentality will leave you exposed to breaches and exploits.
The eventual decommissioning retirement of old technology and services is something that needs to be planned from the start and managed throughout the lifecycle.

Human firewalls avoid throwing out sensitive data, important information and our crown jewels with our old tech junk.

Day 3: Tuesday

Introducing: Sara Z. aka "The Road Warrior"

Tuesdays are for Tacos #tacotuesday. Today we follow the road warrior marketing and sales executive Sara Z. She is on the go and earning frequent flier miles at a record-setting pace while she travels for business and sometimes for pleasure.

Her career takes her to different cities each week, so she is accustomed to being mobile and working remotely. Her office is the airport, coffee shop or hotel she passes through during her travels.

She does not have the network security perimeter firewalls and intrusion protection systems of her corporate offices, so she must be extra diligent during her travels.

Professional Networking security

Sara Z. is always expanding her professional network by using the internet and professional social network sites to form new relationships, connections and network.

She has been using social networks and media sites for well over a decade since her days in high school, college and all throughout her professional career, so she knows how to create her profile, sync her address book, start making connections and develop her professional network.

A few topics are covered in this scenario:
Unfriend
Oversharing
Privacy
Phishing

What should Sara be concerned about in this scenario?

Professionals such as Sara use social networking services to network with new contacts, reconnect with former colleagues, maintain current relationships, promote their business or project and participate in industry discussions.

Some services are positioned as a professional networking site with profiles that reveal a person's resume, email address, phone number, job history, recommendations and group membership.

Cybercriminals abuse the information to find vulnerabilities and launch attacks.

How can you build your human firewall and avoid making the same mistakes?

Here's how:

Step 1. Do not overshare your personal information on professional social networks. Crooks can gather enough personal information from professional social networks to steal your identity.

Criminals can also use the information to impersonate you to launch an attack on your contacts and connections.

Step 2. Protect your ass-ets! Digital assets spread out across the many social network sites can make tracking your assets difficult and provide an opportunity for criminals.

Inventory what information and personal data is stored on each site. Sites may save and store answers to security or password reminder questions, email, credit card, personal storage and document sharing tools that contain sensitive documents like your resume and references.

Step 3. Break the link! Social network apps will often request access to your address book to help you build connections.

This process can get very dangerous if you give access to your personal or professional address book and creates a bad habit of trusting third parties. Do not let social network sites or apps connect to your address book, email, photos or any other services that may contain sensitive information.

Review settings frequently to ensure you did not accidently add permission during a new install or upgrade.

Step 4. You're fired! Professional social network sites are great for connecting and networking, but they can also get you fired from your job.

Most employers have a social media policy which may include limits on what you can post on your social network. Many employers also monitor social networks for employee abuse, information leaks, slander and bad comments.

Also, refrain from using your work email address on your profile since this will likely increase spam, phishing and your employer may also monitor email communications and see all the new job leads and recruiters emailing you.

Step 5. Maintain at least a little privacy! The whole point of professional social networking sites is making new connections which are hard to do if no one can see your profile.

Review the site's privacy settings, for profile access set to registered users only and go a step further and limit access to first and second connections.

This will keep your profile from appearing in internet search engines where anyone (including cybercriminals) can view your information.

Step 6. A big bullseye on your head! From the start, you're a target for cybercriminals and hackers, but once you develop a large following and become a social media influencer, you will have a big fat bullseye on your head.

Make sure you are using a unique and strong password for your account, do not share your credentials with an assistant or family members and add multi-factor authentication to your account.

Most of the popular sites have all had data breaches in the past, so I also suggest you start changing your password at least once a year.

Step 7. Your account will be deactivated if you do not immediately.... You have a new connection request from the CEO... You must change your password.... And many more phishing emails are waiting in your inbox!

Hackers and social engineers use fake social networking emails to lure you into giving up your usernames and passwords. Social Networking opens the floodgates for spam and phishing emails.

Step 8. Hindsight is 20/20! Security was often an afterthought when professional networking and social media apps and sites were developed.

Outdated, rogue, unlicensed and obsolete apps may have unpatched vulnerabilities and are no longer supported and should be removed. Privacy settings are updated with each new and changed state, federal and international regulation.

Keep your apps updated with auto update and check back on privacy settings on a regular basis.

Online Harassment security

Sara is very good at her job and successful which has attracted praise from her peers but also some envy.

Sara did not think much of the jealousy until recently when there were some unsavory comments on an industry blog site from an imposter posing as Sara.

The fake post also caused a flurry of angry comments and emails which continued for weeks. Eventually, the fake profile and comments were removed after Sara contacted the website, but the entire process was time-consuming and frightening since it could happen again.

Sara is now on a mission to clean up her digital-footprint and ensure this does not happen again.

A few topics are covered in this scenario:
Digital Cleanup
Search Engines
Privacy Settings
Password Reuse

What should Sara be concerned about in this scenario?

Cyberbullying and online harassment affect people of all ages. It is vital to understand your rights, when and where to get help.

Cleaning up your digital footprint and online reputation is always important but becomes even more imperative when harassers and bully's aim to tarnish your digital brand and reputation.

Potential future employers, your family, your network, community and the entire world have access to digital footprints.

Your digital footprint can make a lasting impression and you may not have a chance to explain a hacked account, malicious impersonator or false information, so it is critical to proactively manage your digital footprint.

How can you build your human firewall and avoid making the same mistakes?

Here's how:

Step 1. G Rated! Remove, delete, deactivate accounts and take down any inappropriate content that you can control.

Old photos that were taken in poor character moments, blog comments in bad taste and others that may be perceived as poor taste must be dealt with and not ignored since they will never go away.

This is true if you are in a position of a public figure, role model, coach or teacher. If you can control it, then remove it before someone else misuses the material.

Step 2. Don't go too far without HR! Utilize your company's human resources and legal department for assistance. This is not the time to get embarrassed or just ignore the situation and hope it goes away.

Use all your available resources to investigate and resolve the problem before it gets any worse. This is even truer when the coworkers are the potential suspects and bully.

Step 3. Rage but do not engage! Stay calm and not under any circumstances reply or respond to posting or messages from impersonators and cyberbullies.

Responding will just provoke the person or people behind the hateful campaign and make matters worse. If the person happens to work down the hall from you try and avoid a shouting match or physical altercation without HR or a UFC referee on hand.

Step 4. Defense with Evidence! Take screenshots and print copies for evidence keeping.

This should be done immediately and include dates and locations of the material. You want to have proof of the issue and a timeline of the information.

You may need the information in the future and for years to come if the negative information or impersonator comes back.

Step 5. Call the Cops! The police and law enforcement have the tools to track down harassers and cyberbullies.

Get law enforcement involved immediately if there are any threats of violence or other sinister actions. The police should also be alerted of the situation if race, religion, age, veterans and disability are the subject of the harassment.

Step 6. Protect the brand! Your name and reputation is your own personal brand and you must protect it at all costs.

It's impossible to monitor all the social networks, blogs and message boards for malicious activity but some solutions and services can help.

Do an internet search for "social media monitoring" for the latest options and reviews. Many include automated alerts and removal requests.

Remote Access security

Skies the limits for Sara, literally she is in the sky a few times a week traveling to clients. Coffee shops, hotel lobbies, and airports have become her office.

She typically connects back to home base using a mobile hotspot but also uses various wireless networks during her travels.

Her company IT department installed an antivirus program and patches her laptop when she is back in the office.

A few topics are covered in this scenario:
Man-in-the-Middle
Burner Devices
Encryption
Shoulder Surfers

What should Sara be concerned about in this scenario?

The mobile workforce is growing rapidly, and corporate technology and security teams struggle to secure employees behind the walls and firewalls of the corporate office and network.

Mobile and remote access workers are under attack at the locations they frequent the most. Cybercriminals target coffeeshops, hotels, conferences and even airplanes because these are the locations executives work when outside the office and its security perimeter.

How can you build your human firewall and avoid making the same mistakes?

Here's how:

Step 1. Rack up those backups! When you travel with devices they tend to get banged up, lost or stolen so backing up data is a must.

Most people do not consider backups until they lose data to corrupt hardware or worse, ransomware. Manual backups can be time-consuming and error prone, but thankfully there are inexpensive solutions for personal, family and small business usage.

Step 2. If you store, be sure to secure it. If you store your passwords on your devices (or in a physical notebook) you can get in big trouble if the notebook or device is lost, stolen or broken during your travels.

Passwords protect your accounts and information which is the reason why you need to protect your passwords. Stop storing your passwords in spreadsheets named secret-passwords, in address book contact cards, in documents with weak security, in a notebook in your desk or backpack, on a note under your keyboard, in your web browsers save password feature, and anywhere else that they may easily be located and compromised.

Consider using a local or cloud password vault or manager that also requires a strong password and multi-factor authentication.

Step 3. Preflight patching! Before your preflight check-in do some pre-flight patching. Operating systems can quickly fall behind on security patches which will leave the devices vulnerable to threats and attacks.

Mobile devices are even more susceptible because they are on the move and connecting to many networks in their travels.

Using auto updates reduces the chances of your operating system missing patches and mitigates the risk of exploitation. Run patches on devices and software before you travel.

Step 4. Travel tech prep checklist! You probably spent hours or days on your itinerary and packing the right swag for your travels so take a few more minutes and prep your technology for the journey ahead.

Consider removing sensitive data from your devices before you take them on the road. Consider the worst-case scenarios of losing the devices and you may reconsider taking your accounting software or recent tax return on your trip.

Step 5. Last minute holiday shopping! Avoid doing your shopping, banking or accessing any other sensitive information while traveling and connecting to untrusted networks.

You have no control over the security on these untrusted networks or the other devices connected to the networks. It's very easy for the bad guys to create bogus evil twin wireless networks to impersonate your favorite coffee shop, hotel, airport and local public wireless network to lure you on to the network so they can eavesdrop on your communication.

Avoid public and untrusted wireless networks and if you must connect to one of these networks make sure you have a private or personal VPN installed to secure your traffic and reduce the risk.

Step 6. You're forgetful but your devices remember everything! Your devices remember the wireless networks they connected to in the past and will automatically connect to the same networks again when in range.

If auto-connect or auto-join is enabled, your devices may connect to even fake networks using familiar names such as the name of popular coffee shops, hotels and others. Remove the saved networks and disable the auto feature.

Step 7. You will cry the blues when you get bluejacked! There are new Bluetooth exploits all the time and we won't get into the long list of threats or technical details.

If you are using Bluetooth while out traveling the world you are potentially exposing yourself to a host of unwanted exploits and unauthorized access to your devices.

Keep your devices patched and updated with the latest software version and disable Bluetooth when it's not in use.

Step 8. Bed bugs may not be the worst thing you can bring home from your backpacking trip around Europe.

Laptops, smartphones and devices used during your travels can be compromised. Your phone and other devices may pick up malware if you connect with public networks abroad.

Update your security software, perform several scans and change your passwords on all devices on your return home.

Step 9. Hostile territory! If you know you're traveling to a part of the world that is renowned for hacking tourists, politicians and business professionals as they pass through the airports, hotels and coffee shops of the fine city, you should consider using burner or loaner devices.

You want to have the least amount of sensitive data on the loaner device so there is little to nothing to steal and the device can be reformatted when you return to home base.

Identity Theft security

Sara Z. is proactive in developing not only her own career but also giving back to her industry. She is a member of several industry associates and peer groups where she mentors junior members and serves on the board of managers.

She is also a speaker at conferences and writes for newsletters and other industry announcements. Her bio and information are typically distributed with publications, invitations to the events and is listed on the websites.

Sara's career is taking her into the world of public figures and her professional and personal life and information is likely to be targeted by cybercriminals.

A few topics are covered in this scenario:
Credit Freeze
Credit Reports
ID Monitoring
Support

What should Sara be concerned about in this scenario?

You do not have to be a Hollywood celebrity or politician to be a public figure. Personal security and safety can be compromised by posting certain types of information on the internet or publications.

Your participation at an event is revealing that you will be away from home and increases the risk that your home will be burglarized.

You may also risk the safety of your family or children by posting personal details in your bio information on a public website.

How can you build your human firewall and avoid making the same mistakes?

Here's how:

Step 1. Pay now or pay later! Identity monitoring will cost you a few hundred bucks a year, but it is priceless if it prevents a very costly identity theft incident.

There are many services available, so you want to do some homework to find a service that has a comprehensive program that includes social security, medical records, address change, credit monitoring and repair assistance if your identity does get stolen.

Step 2. Pull the alarm! If you have a large following and contact list, you will want to alert everyone immediately if you have a breach that can jeopardize their safety.

Hackers will often use your email account to pivot other attacks and distribute malicious software by emailing your contacts.

Send a warning email to friends and family letting them know that if they've received a suspicious email, text, attachment, and even phone calls from you or regarding you, it should be deleted and ignored.

Step 3. Left out! This is a case where your family won't complain about being left out. Do not include information such as your child's name, school, activities, or details in your bio or profile.

No one in your professional network needs to know you coach little Bart's Springfield elementary school soccer team. The information can easily be misused and create a dangerous situation for your family and children.

Step 4. Freeze out identity thieves! Freeze your credit to restrict access to your credit report and to make it difficult to open new accounts without your authorization.

Creditors will not issue a new line of credit or open a new account without reviewing your credit report. Remember this only protects from opening new accounts and your existing accounts still need proactive monitoring.

Step 5. The price of fame! The publicity and fame will draw the cybercriminals and identity thieves so get ready for the spam, phish and smishing. Bad guys know people love a sensational headline, catchy phrase, free stuff or a bargain.

Clickbait can be anything from a news headline, link in an email message, a clever ad campaign or that free donut link on your favorite blog or social media site.

Step 6. KISS (Keep It Simple Stupid) does not apply to password complexity. A unique long string of 12 or more random characters is still the best password defense.

Don't waste your time coming up with a fancy new passcode, instead use a random password generator or password vault.

Don't fool yourself into believing you have the uncrackable password formula and the cyber-jerks will never get your passwords.

The bad guys have invested more time and money into cracking and social engineering your passwords that your "special code" of swapping letters with numbers or symbols has already been exposed and doesn't stand a chance.

Step 7. Use the free customer service support and helpdesk to assist with the initial setup and new accounts.

Also, revisit old accounts and ask for a review of new security features. Prepare to spend time on all your accounts, healthcare, credit card, driver's license, passport, email addresses, home addresses and your alert preferences.

The systems and services can only monitor the information you provide so to get the maximum coverage and return on investment make a checklist.

Homeowner security

Sara's career takes her away from home on a frequent basis, so she has her neighbors keep an eye on her home while she is away and contact her if there is an emergency.

She lives in a safe area of town and is not overly concerned with security, but she sets her lights on a timer for peace of mind while she is away.

In the past she had a professional home monitoring service but when the contract expired she did not renew the service.

A few topics are covered in this scenario:
Home Monitoring
Security Cameras
Professional Services
Mail Delivery

What should Sara be concerned about in this scenario?

Security starts at home and requires ongoing maintenance. Know your surroundings, your neighborhood and your block.

Meet your neighbors and develop a neighborhood watchdog program to lookout for each other and report issues. Broadcasting that no one is home or saying that you're traveling for an extended period is asking for trouble.

Public sharing any kind of personal or work travel information is highly dangerous, and you may unknowingly be doing it right now in your social network, voicemail, email signature and others.

Home safety is critical for the entire family and sharing travel information with friends and working relationships can potentially be intercepted and exploited by criminals.

How can you build your human firewall and avoid making the same mistakes?

Here's how:

Step 1. Back to the basics! Physical security is an important area of security control. Locking doors, windows and garage doors are a must.

Install deadbolts and secure door frames, secure sheds and yards that may contain tools that could be used to break into your home.

Avoid the spare key under the doormat or under the large rock in the garden because the criminals will find it and use it.

Step 2. Full house! Always make your home seems occupied to deter burglars and home invaders. Something as simple as keeping the radio on can prevent a burglary.

Place timers on lights in different rooms to give the appearance of activity. Install motion sensing lighting around the perimeter of the home.

Step 3. Landscape! If your grass is growing too high, it may signal criminals no one is home here.

Trees, shrubs and bushes can become overgrown and potentially camouflage a burglar breaking into a window or door hidden behind the overgrown landscaping. Hire a local landscaper to provide ongoing maintenance.

Step 4. Sign of the times. Home security signs are a great way to deter burglars and an actual home security system may catch the home invaders.

Cameras and a video recording system are great detective tools for evidence and having cameras in plain sight will also deter criminals.

Step 5. Oh oh it's magic! Update your OOO settings, so your Out of Office (OOO) does not reply to everyone and anyone who emails you including the spammers, social engineers and hackers.

Also, remove any personal information that can be misused. There is no legitimate reason why your OOO should mention you are away or have limited access to email since this little bit of information can be exploited.

Step 6. On hold! Put your mail delivery on hold and put a stop to automatic recurring deliveries while you are away from home.

A stack of mail, boxes and newspapers at your front door will attract the wrong attention and advertise that no one is home.

Step 7. Get informed! The USPS offers Informed Delivery service which sends you an email preview of your mail and package tracking. With Informed Delivery, you can review daily images of the exterior of the mail and package tracking numbers.

You should also sign up your home address before someone else does. Someone can potentially view your incoming mail envelope images and determine if any items are worth stealing from your mailbox.

Tuesday Takeaways:

The world is a big place that should be seen and explored. Our technology, sensitive information, prized possessions and assets are often along for the ride as we travel.

It is essential to understand the threats and the risk we undertake during leisure and work-related travels since the friendly skies may contain a few dark clouds.

When considering your assets consider the non-tangible, your reputation and identity should be regarded as priceless.

Your reputation is your personal brand which can travel way beyond the borders of your town, state and country without ever setting foot on an airplane.

Our interconnected world allows our reputation, identity and brand to span the globe which exposes us to threats from everywhere.

Human firewall building is protecting your personal brand and identity, you must make it a high priority along with your other more obvious crown jewels.

Day 4: Wednesday

Introducing: Marc L. aka "The Golden Years"

Wednesday is halfway to the weekend #humpday and our Humpday hero is none other than Marc L. He is our hero because he made it to retirement while the rest of us are still in the daily grind.

He may be retired from the workforce, but that does not mean the cybercriminals have crossed him off their list of targets. Marc L. is a prize target for cyber-goons who are looking to exploit his identity, steal his retirement savings and hijack his computing power to launch more attacks.

Email security

Before Marc retired his former employer performed an annual cybersecurity awareness training for employees and Marc failed the phishing exercise every time but he learned from his mistakes.

When he receives a fake (phish) email from Healthcare administration requesting sensitive information he refrains from clicking the link in the message and sends a reply to the sender "keep trying you cyber jerks" to let the bad guys know not to mess with him.

How many readers also have the urge to give scammers a piece of their mind?

A few topics are covered in this scenario:
Email Scams
Cyber Awareness
Identity Theft
Phishing

What should Marc be concerned about in this scenario?

Everyone has some experience one way or another with cybersecurity and technology. That experience can be from work-related cyber awareness training or the hard way of learning from the horrible experience of having your identity stolen, spam phishing email or a ransomware malware type event.

It is critical to keep learning and stay proactive with your personal threat protection. Cybercriminals are evolving, data breaches are a regular event and new vulnerabilities are discovered which creates additional threats to your crown jewels. Keep learning and training!

How can you build your human firewall and avoid making the same mistakes?

Here's how:

Step 1. Do not share your medical data, healthcare information or Medicare card number with anyone. You will never have to pay for a new Medicare or Health Care card or provide personal or sensitive information to receive a new card.

Be suspicious of any unsolicited email communications claiming to be related to Medicare or healthcare.

Step 2. Healthcare providers and Medicare will never send an email to collect your personal information. A red flag that they are fraudulent scammers is when they request your private information and claim to be an "Agent".

Contact your healthcare provider directly to submit any personal information.

Step 3. Scammers do not discriminate against age. Beware the scammer emails claiming to offer unbelievable "to good to be true" returns on your investments and retirement savings.

Cybercriminals will go far to scam you out of your money, even creating fake websites that mimic legitimate investment brokerage websites with secure logins and stock watch lists.

Make sure you check with financial regulators before investing in any financial institution or investments.

Step 4. Denial! Don't ever say "It won't happen to me." You are a target, you open emails, click links and if you don't proactively protect yourself, you will endure the time consuming and the costly aftermath of a breach or identity theft recovery.

Realize that you are an attractive target for hackers. In the event you do get ripped off, be sure to seek out help from family, friends and law enforcement.

The bad guys are hoping you will be too ashamed to get help. Get help!

Step 5. Identify the threats and vulnerabilities to your assets. Email is an asset because it contains a wealth of sensitive information in messages, attachments and address book contacts.

Vulnerabilities can be anything from an old device or operating system no longer supported or your favorite coffee shop's free wireless network. It is critical that you only access your email from secured devices and trusted networks.

Step 6. Unsubscribe! Do not use the unsubscribe link in spam emails. Do not reply to spammers, for any reason.

Unsubscribe buttons often ask for more information such as name, email and more. Your reply or unsubscribe will provide evidence you are a real person that opens emails and the spammers will just increase activity.

Step 7. URGENT! Stay calm and think about it before quickly jumping into action.

Usually, there is an urgent matter that requires immediate attention, such as a failure to login will have your account closed or your mailbox is full, and you can no longer get new messages.

These urgent messages request you to click a link and login to validate your account. Hover or mouseover email links (or links in documents) to view the actual destination. Do this for all links, even from trusted sources.

Step 8. Dead links! Type in the website name in your browser or search engine rather than clicking on a link in an email.

You cannot trust links at all, especially unsolicited emails. If in doubt, do not enter your credentials, log into their webpage directly not through the email link.

Step 9. Never ever give out personal information based on an email request or an unsolicited phone call.

Go to the company website to obtain the correct phone number and never trust the contact information in the email signature.

Step 10. You are not the Smithsonian! Unless you're a historian or have some legal reasons, you need to stop keeping every email from the beginning of time in your inbox.

In the event your email account is compromised the bad guys will likely find very usual information in your old emails to launch additional attacks and further damages.

Perform mailbox cleanups periodically to delete old messages and make sure you also include your sent items as well as the inbox.

Step 11. Are you still hot for Hotmail? It's time to delete all those old email accounts that you no longer use and may not even remember the passwords to access.

No longer popular may also be less secure email platforms which could still contain your confidential information such as contacts, email attachments, passwords and answers to security questions.

Shut them down before the bad guys break-in and start doing some damage to your identity and reputation.

Step 12. Automatic is only going to get you hacked faster. Disable automatic image loading in emails. Applications do not always come configured for strong security by default and email systems that automatically download message images is a perfect example.

Just opening one single pixel is enough to send a message back to bad guys that you are a living breathing human who is curious, and they will launch additional attacks to see what else you're dumb enough to do.

Step 13. Bad grammar gets the hammer! Online or email scams are no longer identifiable by poor grammar and spelling mistakes.

With all the grammar apps and spell checkers, you would think the cyber-goons could win a spelling-bee by now. Keep a lookout for obvious spelling and grammar mistakes.

Step 14. Typo Squats! You will not find anyone doing sets of typo squats in the gym, but you will find malicious cybercriminals registering domain names similar to the names of legitimate sites and services.

The typo-squatters are hoping you login with your credentials on their fake websites so they can steal your information, identity and more.

Software security

Marc knows he needs to use an antivirus program to keep his computer safe from malware and viruses, but he just bought a new computer which came with a 90-day trial version so to save a few bucks he is going to wait for the trial to near expiration before purchasing.

The trial version is fully operational with just one annoyance, a frequent pop-up reminder to purchase the program before the pending expiration but Marc doesn't mind and quickly clicks the pop-up window away.

A few topics are covered in this scenario:
Trial Versions
New Computers
Pop-ups
Fake Antivirus

What should Marc be concerned about in this scenario?

Security software such as antivirus, malware removers and personal firewalls have been around forever and are part of having a defense in depth model for protection.

Using the layered approach of having multiple security tools running creates extra security and resiliency for when one system or application fails, another will hopefully succeed.

Personal security software is relatively inexpensive and can be found for free, but it is also impersonated by cybercriminals so make sure you are getting it from a legitimate source.

There are many known malicious applications and malware that impersonate antivirus software so they can spy on your computer and exfiltrate the data.

How can you build your human firewall and avoid making the same mistakes?

Here's how:

Step 1. Fake Out! Fake antivirus software has become a big profit maker for cybercriminals. Stick to well-known name brand antivirus endpoint protection solutions.

Another tip is to purchase a block of licenses of 5 or more for the entire family to save big bucks and don't let the services auto-renew. You typically get the largest discount on a new purchase.

Step 2. Clean house! Clean out all the junk, old software, trial software, obsolete software and hardware from your technology inventory.

Remove the free antivirus software that expired and has not been updated in years. Software conflicts can occur, and that old free trial that came installed on your computer may interfere with your updated paid antimalware and antivirus protection software.

Step 3. Don't be late with an antivirus update! Make sure your security software is updating, performing regularly scheduled scans and all available features are working properly.

Most antivirus software comes bundled with a security suite of endpoint protection including a host firewall. Use all available tools and resources.

Step 4. Your Antivirus company is not going to call you! Tech support scams are common these days and often use current news events in the scam campaigns.

Unsolicited calls from popular software vendors or website virus pop-up alerts warning you have a virus or security issues are likely scams.

Never accept an offer for unsolicited remote tech support from a caller or email.

Step 5. Don't let your browser be a cookie monster. Clear your cache or set your browser to auto delete the contents when you close the application.

Review privacy and security settings in your browser to accept, block cookies and activate tracking protection to block online trackers.

Step 6. Pop goes the weasel! Use a pop-up blocker to limit ads and tracking software. The pop-up windows, pop-ups and pop-unders are windows that appear automatically without your permission.

Pop-up blockers are also called Ad blockers and Privacy blockers are typically included in your modern web browsers but can also be added as a trusted browser extension.

They help reduce unwanted ads that vary in size from small to covering the whole screen. Some pop-ups open on top of the current window, while others appear underneath (pop-under).

Step 7. Everyone could use a little support! Setting up security software can be confusing, but legitimate software vendors offer support and assistance with install and configuration.

Just double check the phone number before you make the call. Fraudsters are known to register numbers similar to legitimate software companies and also advertise offers of tech support for popular software with the hopes you call the wrong number. Triple check the phone number!

Social Network security

To keep in touch with friends, family and grandchildren, Marc L. has recently started using social networking.

He quickly joins a few groups, his former school alumni and reconnects with former classmates. Within a few weeks, he is very active commenting, liking, playing games, entering lotteries, tagging photos, and sending direct messages.

He really enjoys the ease of access from his computer and smartphone while on the move. Keeping in touch with friends and family is a great benefit of social networking sites and is enjoyed by people of all ages.

A few topics are covered in this scenario:
Privacy Settings
Geolocation
Personal Information
Sweepstakes and Lotteries

What should Marc be concerned about in this scenario?

The internet and social networking are entertaining for all ages, but it is also a risk for people of all ages. Cybercriminals and social engineers have developed profiles and lures for people of all ages as well.

Casino games, lotteries, sweepstakes, online bingo, and countless others are used to deceive people, especially older users, into believing that they have won a prize.

This is very common and scammers use these techniques to obtain sensitive personal information and access to financial accounts.

How can you build your human firewall and avoid making the same mistakes?

Here's how:

Step 1. Jackpot! You play online games and enter the lottery to win big but it's the cybercriminals who hit the jackpot.

Do not be tricked into providing personal information to scammers running fake online casino games and lotteries.

Scammers often provide claim forms to request personal information such as social security numbers and bank account information to deliver your winnings. There are no winnings and you will lose your personal information and more.

Step 2. Delivery fee! You thought the delivery fee was too expensive for food delivery, then wait until you see the delivery and processing fee for your lottery and sweepstakes winnings.

Legitimate lottery and games do not charge a delivery and processing fee, but scammers will ask you to pay a percentage of your winnings by money wire or another financial transaction, so they can deliver your prize. Scam!

Step 3. Block the Bots on Social Networks. Social Bots or SocBots send fake friend requests, once connected the bots may spam friends, spread malicious links, advocate potentially harmful ideas and gather information.

Remember to check security settings but also remember that friends can see your activity and other connections so do not connect to every friend request, only connect with people you really know.

Step 4. Keep it in the Family! When discussing family matters or the family business, make it clear to family members that the best way of communicating is over the phone or email and not posting on social networks.

Family members new to social media may not understand the difference between public and private conversations so make sure you educate mom before her feelings get hurt when you must delete her public posting in which she asks how your weird rash is doing.

Don't hesitate to remove something that is too personal for fear of hurting family members feelings.

Step 5. Give me back my son! This one reminds me of the Mel Gibson movie Ransom.

Using the information found on your social media profile the scammers and con-artists may pose as kidnappers and call, text or send messages to urge you to wire money immediately for the release of your family member.

The calls typically coincide with the family member being unavailable or traveling out of the country. Thanks to email out of office auto replies and social media status updates and geolocators it's easy to find out when someone is traveling or away.

Their goal is to trick you into sending money before you can reach the family member and realize it's a scam.

Step 6. Charity starts at home! Scammers use real news and events to create a fake charity and fundraising campaigns on social networks, websites and spam emails.

Fraudsters use bogus profiles that will steer victims to non-social media managed websites to attempt to collect data and money from potential victims. Research the charity before contributing to a potential scam.

Password security

Marc L. knows password best practices from his former employer's cybersecurity awareness training and that passwords are one of the first lines of defense.

In the past he reused passwords and had one password for all his accounts and if he ever had to change it he would update the number at the end.

After lots of training he now knows he needs to use a unique and complex password for all his accounts, but he is very fortunate to have several children, grandchildren and pets' names to help him create unique, clever and memorable passwords that he can remember.

A few topics are covered in this scenario:
Passwords
Multi-Factor

Password Managers
Sharing Passwords

What should Marc be concerned about in this scenario?

You can't spell password without the word ass and most of us have been an ass when it comes to password security.

Since the start of modern civilization people have relied on passwords and unfortunately used poor password hygiene such as easy to guess passwords, common words as passwords, poorly hidden passwords, reused passwords, shared passwords, written passwords on notepads.

The list can go on and on but I think everyone gets the point about passwords. Passwords are a necessary evil of our daily lives and the average person likely has more passwords and credentials than they could ever remember in their head at least.

This is why the bad habits of writing passwords down and reusing the same password across many different systems and sites have become so common.

In recent years there have been breaches of hundreds of sites ranging from social media, dating, shopping, email, and others in which passwords were leaked and used downstream in other breaches because people reused the same password.

Our passwords are one of the first lines of defense in our human firewall so let's strengthen our password muscle.

How can you build your human firewall and avoid making the same mistakes?

Here's how:

Step 1. Passwords are the first line of defense and not only should the password be complex, but the password protection and storage should also be complex so do not make it easy for criminals or prying eyes to easily infiltrate your assets with unprotected passwords.

Step 2. Don't let history repeat itself because you have plain text passwords in old emails. Some sites, services and people still send plain text passwords in emails (shaking my head and saying no no no).

Delete those old password emails, password reset emails and any other email related to credentials or sensitive information so when the terrible day comes that your email is breached there will hopefully be less damage.

Step 3. Passwords are like a cold winter day so layer up for protection. Add multi-factor authentication, two-step verification, 2FA, MFA, and all other commonly used terms to describe adding a second verification to your password sign-in.

This second step may save your butt if your credentials are exposed in a breach or you are tricked into giving up your credentials.

Most sites do not require adding a second step, so be a diligent and proactive human firewall by adding the second step yourself.

Step 4. Running out of passwords! Let's face it, you're just not creative enough to come up with unique and complex passwords for all your accounts and remembering them all is an impossible task.

Start using a good online password manager also called a password vault to store and generate strong passwords.

Don't cheap out and use a free password manager, buy or subscribe to the paid version for a few dollars and activate two-factor authentication to secure your crown jewels further.

Step 5. Autofill will drain your bank account! Web browsers are highly targeted by cybercriminals because they often save sensitive information such as credentials, passwords and payment card numbers.

Browsers are also susceptible to vulnerabilities as user's browse the vast internet and are exposed to its many threats.

Disable autofill, credit card and password saving features and enable automatic updates.

Step 6. Get real about passwords! Just don't use actual real words as passwords. Using common words will leave your accounts susceptible to dictionary attacks.

Cybercriminals have tools that can automatically crack passwords made of common words and even words spelled backward.

Step 7. Surf's up! Social engineers use clever tactics besides technology hacks, cracking tools and phishing email to obtain your passwords.

A social engineer may stake out your favorite coffee shop to wait for the moment when you type in your passwords on your laptop or smartphone.

By shoulder surfing, they can look over your shoulder to see you type in a password or use a smartphone camera to record it.

Step 8. Eighth is great! Eight is great but 12 or more is even better. The longer the password the harder it will be to crack, shoulder surf and guess.

You are much more secure using a long passphrase of words that only you understand such as 1willLovetoEatPizza4Ever which may or may not be true but makes for a very difficult password to crack.

Job Search security

Marc L. has been retired for about a year already and is looking for new ways to stay active outside his usual daily routine, so he has started to explore working part-time and volunteer work as options to stay active and help the community.

He performs a few searches on the web and he quickly finds several job websites, volunteer and charity fundraising in his area and a few that also allow him to work from his home.

He decides to apply to a couple of the roles and post his resume to a few of the job boards and within a few days his phone is ringing with new leads.

A few topics are covered in this scenario:
Job Websites
Recruiters
Charities
Social Security

What should Marc be concerned about in this scenario?

Way back when I was young (really showing my age here) we would use the local newspapers classifieds help wanted section to find jobs.

Sometimes to apply a high-tech fax machine was required but these days there are dozens of job boards and resume websites for job seekers and recruiters.

Your resume likely contains your full legal name, home address, phone number, email address, work history and education and if you recall the answers to some of your financial service website security questions you will likely find some answers in your resume.

Cybercriminals love using low-tech hacks to steal your stuff and publicly available resumes on job websites are easy-pickings.

You may have the best intentions of finding a new job to increase your livelihood and fortune, but you may also make yourself vulnerable to a breach or identity theft.

How can you build your human firewall and avoid making the same mistakes?

Here's how:

Step 1. All about the fake out! If the job seems too good to be true or you already answered an unsolicited call with someone from the human resources department at the company you really want to work for, it's perfectly fine to say politely please provide me with your contact information and I will call you back.

Call back at a more convenient time and of course that time is after you verified the job is legit. Contact the company directly using the information on the company website.

Step 2. Help me help you. Don't give any away personal or sensitive information in your resume, to the recruiters and human resource staff.

They should never ask for your social security number, a copy of a driver's license or passport, and any type of payment to secure a job interview.

Step 3. Please complete an application for malware. Another smooth trick exploiting the hard-working job seekers is the using malicious code embedded in fake job applications on bogus job postings or sent from fake recruiters or human resource professionals.

In hopes of a possible new job don't let your guard down and ignore the virus and macro warnings. Always virus scan documents, file attachments and pay attention to macro warnings.

Step 4. Fake Squared. Fake job sites, fake jobs and fake checks. A successful scam involves contacting job seekers using the name of a real company, setting up a video conferencing interview followed by a quick job offer that includes a signing bonus.

The scammer will ask for personal information for tax and banking purposes, but you will never see a dime of signing bonus and likely never hear from the scammer again once they have your information.

Step 5. Don't get wrecked by an e-check! Electronic checking and ACH are very convenient especially for recurring payments and automatic payments from employers.

The initial setup typically requires sharing routing and account numbers which can create a current and future risk.

Beware fake jobs with quick job offers followed by requests for your banking and social security number information.

Step 6. Job bored! Posting a resume to internet job boards for the world to see is a great way to find a new job or have your identity stolen.

If you do post your resume on a public job board, make sure to remove all personal information such as your home address.

I also suggest creating an email address just for job seeking purposes, use a secondary virtual phone number, and consider replacing your full last name with only the first initial.

Step 7. Infectious news! Scammers will attempt to capitalize on current news events such as a major catastrophe or disaster.

Often setting up fake fundraising campaigns or attempting to spread malicious code and malware through email, texts, links, attachments and websites.

Messages titled with breaking news relating to a recent event may contain attachments loaded with a malicious payload or link directed to a video attachment.

If you want to help be sure to go to contact a reputable charity or service provider.

Wednesday Takeaways:

Cybercriminals, hackers, social engineers, scammers and the other malicious threat actors do not discriminate.

Everyone is fair game when it comes to identity theft, financial fraud and other money-making scams.

It is important to understand we are being outmatched by organized crime gangs, government-sponsored hackers and other malicious groups who have created a business model and profit from the crimes they commit and mayhem they cause around the globe.

Even something as selfless and innocent as volunteering or charitable fundraising has been exploited by cybercriminals.

Staying aware and continuously increasing your defenses will reduce your likelihood but breaches are inevitable. To minimize the impact, you must maintain a strong cybersecurity posture which includes regular best practice training and threat awareness.

It is safe to assume that cybercriminals have found a way to exploit and monetize just about everything. When exploring something new do a quick search of cybersecurity threats and risks for whatever the subject you are exploring such as "cybersecurity threats when job searching".

If you are able and willing, you should help others and part of building your human firewall is making cybersecurity an ongoing exercise which you should share and encourage others to participate in.

Day 5: Thursday

Introducing: Shawna G. aka "The Princess Bride"

Thursday is #ThirstyThursday and our thirsty Thursday character is none other than the recent newlyweds Shawna G. and her new hubby John W.

Our newlyweds have recently tied the knot and are excited to start their life together. The couple met through a dating app a couple of years ago and have been inseparable ever since.

Together they survived the mayhem and craziness of planning a large wedding and are excited for the future which includes an upcoming lavish and relaxing honeymoon around Europe.

Maybe we can tag along on the honeymoon for extra security.

Life Event security

Shawna and John spent the last 12 months planning the perfect wedding which included a wedding website, wedding announcements, gift registries, several wedding vendors, event planners and a wedding dance coach.

The couple published a wedding announcement in several local and national newspapers and created a wedding website with a blog for friends and family to follow, share photos and stories. Seems like a perfect fairytale wedding.

A few topics are covered in this scenario:
Oversharing
Personal Information
Third-parties
Occasions

What should Shawna be concerned about in this scenario?

Don't let your guard down as you celebrate a joyous occasion or gloomy day. Criminals will turn your occasions into opportunities.

Wedding websites and announcements can contain a large amount of personal information about you and your future spouse, family members and friends.

The information in announcements, websites, newspaper publications and other sources may provide criminals the addresses, mother's maiden name, and birth dates which can be used to guess passwords, steal identities and burglarize empty homes.

Depending on your privacy settings, even social media activity can be risky.

How can you build your human firewall and avoid making the same mistakes?

Here's how:

Step 1. Life event hacking! Do not overshare private information during life events. Life events can be unknowingly broadcast online without your authorization.

Publishing a birth announcement, marriage or obituary to a local newspaper will also be published to the paper's online website and could also be distributed to the newspaper's national partners.

Step 2. Announcing no one is home! Public broadcasting of weddings, funerals, births and others can provide crooks enough information to determine where you live and when you are not going to be home.

Be cautious when making an occasion public information or you may become a burglary victim.

Step 3. Use a unique and super strong password to access your service providers online portals and cloud services.

Avoid creating an account and credentials with a meaningful password that can be guessed from information on your wedding website or other shared information.

Step 4. Defacement! Make sure you use a reputable hosting provider for your wedding website that includes modern security features.

Configure the security and privacy settings of your wedding website as soon as possible. Activate the multi-factor authentication and access alerts to reduce the chance of compromised account damages.

Some providers also allow IP address or location whitelisting which is helpful if you always access the services from the same network and locations.

Step 5. To encrypt or not to encrypt! It all depends on how important and sensitive the data is. Just assume the photo sharing cloud provider and your data is going to be breached.

If you are backing up photos or tax returns or other super sensitive data, you better password protect (encrypt) before sending to the cloud.

Step 6. Plan B! Have a backup plan if you are hosting important, sensitive, one of a kind data such as once in a lifetime wedding photos and videos or (IP) Intellectual Property in the cloud.

If the provider suffers a breach, ransomware attack, or even discontinues services for any other reason, you will need a copy of your data to move to a new provider.

Yes, services shut down, retire, merge, get sold, get hacked, become infected with ransomware and much.

Step 7. Get a prenup! Seriously, have you considered what happens to your data when you no longer use the service or delete your account?

Reputable service providers should have a delete all or forget me type option available when you want to discontinue service.

Make sure you consider an exit strategy when choosing online services providers.

Step 8. Fake and bake! There are a lot of vendors involved in planning a special event such as a wedding and fraudsters can use the information gathered from a couples wedding website for scams.

A common scam is a phony invoice requesting payment for wedding services or the venue. One way to identify a fake invoice is if the sender's reply to the email address is from a free email service and not the wedding cake bakery or catering company email domain.

Step 9. Back it up! You spent months planning and have gigabytes of video and pictures to help the memories last a lifetime.

Make sure you have backups of all the important memories. A local backup and a cloud backup copy will help avoid losing the data during a local disaster (fire, flood, etc.) and a cloud service provider incident (ransomware, out of business, etc.)

Personal Information security

Shawna is excited to take her new husband's name and is eager to update her identification such as passport, social security card, credit cards and driver's license before the upcoming honeymoon travels.

She does some research online which quickly points her to several service provider websites and blogs with tips and resources for changing your name.

She is excited to get started, but the list is growing long, so she is contemplating using a name-change service that is advertising on one of the wedding blog sites she frequents.

A few topics are covered in this scenario:
Fake Advertisements
Identity Theft
Social Engineering
Credit Cards

What should Shawna be concerned about in this scenario?

Sensitive and personally identifiable information is highly targeted by criminals and identity thieves. The process of changing personal information potentially provides criminals an opportunity to intercept information using technology and social engineering techniques.

It is more important to be vigilant now and if you decide to use third-party services for assistance, it is critical to vet the service providers and their security practices.

How can you build your human firewall and avoid making the same mistakes?

Here's how:

Step 1. Security over convenience! We all have demands on our time and are looking for ways to delegate our workloads by seeking assistance from service providers.

In some cases, we are giving the service providers authorization to act on our behalf and manage sensitive information, so it is vital to vet providers and perform cybersecurity due diligence reviews of their practices.

Every person and business can get hacked so you need to limit your personal attack surface by only using providers with a strong cybersecurity posture.

Ask about their cybersecurity plan, policies and history of security events.

Step 2. Secure your Social Security Number! You should always monitor your social security information such as earnings, work history and benefits because it will help identify fraud on your account.

Criminals steal a victim's Social Security number to obtain medical benefits, file a fake state or federal tax refund, apply for credit cards and steal your benefits.

Step 3. Out with the old and in with the new. You can get a brand-new social security number if you can provide evidence of abuse or theft.

Consider getting a new SSN if someone has stolen your number, if your number is used by multiple people (this happens when someone uses the wrong number accidently and intentionally) or if you are being harassed or in danger.

Step 4. The traveling credit card! Credit cards sometimes go for walks and travel without us especially after the numbers are stolen in any of the many credit card scams and data breaches. You can request a new credit card number from your bank at any time.

If you have had the same number for years, have had any type of identity breach or been part of a corporate breach you should request a new number immediately.

Step 5. Review the report! At least once a year you should review your credit report for invalid information.

Repairing errors or unauthorized activity on your credit report can take a long time so do not wait until you get declined for an auto or home loan to review your report.

Step 6. Family protection! Identity protection for the whole family is a must have and there are many vendors and service options available.

Companies are offering free services and free trials which require your personal information and like anything free there is usually a hidden cost.

Your personal information is worth a lot more than a free trial or the $20 a month many of the services charge so avoid "free" identity protection services.

Ancestry Search security

The newlyweds had a large wedding and spent time with family members they had not seen in a very long time.

Both were surprised by the large size and diversity of each side of their family which made them want to explore more about their family history and heritage.

They both decided to explore further using online ancestry and family tree websites. Let's hope the couple locate the family jewels and avoid the nuts as they search their family trees online.

A few topics are covered in this scenario:
Genealogy Scams
Fake Experts
Fake Websites
DNA Sites

What should Shawna be concerned about in this scenario?

Ancestry and genealogy sites and services are very popular as people look for ways to explore family history and reconnect with family members.

Scammers set up a fake website with the intention of capturing your financial and personal information as you search for family history.

They develop websites, advertisements and email campaigns to lure people who are interested in ancestral research and tempt them to register in their fake websites.

It can be fascinating tracing your ancestry, finding out about your roots and building a family tree but it can also sometimes lead you into scams.

How can you build your human firewall and avoid making the same mistakes?

Here's how:

Step 1. Hooray for Inheritance! Scammers love delivering good news so don't be surprised when you receive good news about a hefty inheritance waiting for you.

The scammers may even provide an ancestry report of the wealthy relative. There is just one catch and you will have to provide credit card information to prepay for legal and processing fees. Don't be a sucker for the inheritance scam.

Step 2. Phony Baloney! Ancestry and genealogy experts charge high fees and require access to your personal information to perform their research.

Several organizations require members to undertake training and exams before vouching for their expertise.

It's up to you to do the background check on qualifications and experience so do your diligence before you give your money and personal information to an "expert".

Step 3. Family history book! You could save yourself a lot of time if you purchase a family history book instead of doing all the work to create your own.

The problem is the family history book, family coat of arms and family crest are well-known scams designed to lure family history seekers.

Avoid the letters in the mail, bogus online ads and spam emails selling these services. Do your research before using any service provider.

Step 4. Weak link! By now you are aware of the risks of using services and vendors with weak cybersecurity and the same goes for ancestry, genealogy, and family tree service providers.

A recent hack exposed information of 92 million users and it took over 6 months for the company to identify the breach.

Do some research on the security practices and check for recent data breaches in the news before you sign up and share your personal and financial information.

Step 5. Private parts! There are long confusing privacy agreements when you subscribe and share your information with ancestry, genealogy, and family tree services.

There is a lot of private information collected including DNA and there is little control over how that information is used by the profit-making companies.

Recently police have utilized genealogy DNA services to identify suspects and solve cold case crimes which has caused many to debate the potential for invasion of privacy and misuse of the information.

Keep in mind you may be giving away more than just a DNA sample.

Step 6. Pay for FDA! Home DNA tests also claim to reveal health issues and discover genetic secrets that may affect your future health.

The FDA has recently started approving some tests and new updates are coming out all the time. I highly suggest if you have any health concerns you should seek the help of a licensed healthcare provider and a certified professional doctor.

Personal Privacy security

Shawna and John are preparing for their long-awaited honeymoon which is a 14-day tour of Europe. They are beyond excited for the international adventure and have been preparing and packing all week.

The couple has several destinations planned during their trip which also includes a few tours and excursions with local tour guides, but they also plan to explore on their own.

To share the adventure and keep in touch with family the couple is planning to post daily updates of their social media sites.

A few topics are covered in this scenario:

Malicious Countries
Public Wireless
Physical Security
Real-time

What should Shawna be concerned about in this scenario?

A wedding should be a joyous occasion as is any chance to take a vacation and travel. Social media and photo sharing sites allow travelers to share their adventures in real time with friends, family and strangers.

Posting real-time updates, geotagging photos, location tracking, checking-in and other features share your status and location with friends and loved-ones but also with strangers and potential criminals with bad intentions.

How can you build your human firewall and avoid making the same mistakes?

Here's how:

Step 1. Real-time crime time! Do not post your honeymoon pictures while you are away on your honeymoon.

Posting real-time pictures while you're traveling or on a honeymoon may alert crooks that you're away from home.

Wait until you are back home before you post pictures to online photo share sites and social media.

Step 2. Notify your bank! Do not expect a wedding gift or bon voyage from your bank but they will watch your back while you're traveling.

Alert your bank and credit card company when you are traveling outside the country, the dates and locations of your travels. Your bank will note the information on your account to monitor for suspicious activity.

Step 3. Booking it! Be prepared for the tourist traps and a barrage of solicitations for sightseeing tours.

Do your research before you travel and book your tour reservations before you leave home. Make sure you book with secure and reputable companies.

Read reviews and ask your hotel for recommendations.

Step 4. Man-in-the-middle! During your travels, you will come across many opportunities to connect to wireless networks in hotels, airports, cafes and many more places offering free wireless internet access.

You will be very tempted to connect to the networks to save money on roaming and data charges but the cost of repairing a data breach or identity theft will be much costlier.

Only connect to secure trusted networks during your travels and avoid accessing personal information while connected to untrusted networks.

Step 5. Shake shimmer skimmer! Nope, it's not a dance, but criminals will be doing a happy dance when they use shimmers and skimmers to steal your credit and debit card information at ATMs and credit card machines.

The small devices are hard to spot and even wiggling the card reader and keypad may not help.
Try to avoid using ATMs when traveling by planning accordingly and carrying enough cash for your trip.

If you must use an ATM at least use a bank machine and avoid the random ATM machine on the street or storefront.

Step 6. GPS'd! Your phone, apps and your camera with built-in GPS may be giving away your location and allow unauthorized surveillance.

Review the privacy settings to deactivate the geotagging features to avoid public pinpointing of your location, home, and even your travels.

Couples Financial security

Sharing is caring so Shawna and John have begun cohabitating, sharing space and the process of combining finances and financial service accounts.

They have also started setting up their emergency contact information, beneficiary updates and sharing healthcare provider services.

The couple is also setting up a joint email to use for shared accounts and services. They are using a clever password of combined dates that are very special to the couple and no one could ever guess.

A few topics are covered in this scenario:
Password Managers
Email
Browsers
Sharing

What should Shawna be concerned about in this scenario?

Sharing sensitive information and finances may be especially difficult for couples who have different ideas about money management but can be catastrophic if one person has poor cybersecurity hygiene.

Ideally a couple should be comfortable discussing their assets and any history of identity theft or exposure in breaches, but this can be a sensitive subject.

Waiting until you are breached again to have the discussion will be too late. It's better to immediately identify any gaps in either person's security and take steps to repair and maintain human firewall security hygiene.

How can you build your human firewall and avoid making the same mistakes?

Here's how:

Step 1. We can only be as strong as our weakest link and cyber-goons will target your friends, family, co-workers or significant others who may have easy access to your passwords or "crown jewels" so don't share passwords.

Create separate account credentials for each person and each website. If possible limit the access to only the necessary basic level of services.

Step 2. Basic instincts! Apply the strongest cybersecurity practices when securing your accounts and make sure your partner does the same.

Do not let your partner be the weakest link by reusing old passwords for new joint accounts. Use multi-factor authentication, a password manager and prevent malware by using antivirus software.

Request support and training from your financial intuitions. Be sure to include training on available security features and best practices.

Step 3. Bankers box! No, not the cardboard box! Create a new banking and financial services email mailbox for only the new bank accounts, financial activity and alerts.

Just use the new email account for couple related financial activity. Don't click on untrusted communications emails or texts that ask for account information in your other email accounts.

Also, avoid accessing financial accounts using shared computers or open wireless networks and saving passwords in web browsers.

Step 4. Constant contact! Review and update your contact information for financial reasons on a regular basis. If you still have paper copies mailed to an old address or new cards sent to the wrong address, you could be asking for identity theft.

The same is true for phone numbers which may also receive two-factor pin codes or receive text alerts for account activity. Configure the paperless feature if the feature is available.

Step 5. Consolidate! Managing multiple financial accounts can get complicated. Some employers can consolidate previous retirement accounts which is helpful if you switch jobs often.

Consider combining accounts into less services providers and maintain at least two for redundancy.

Step 6. Your love is bad medicine! Your partner may tell you this if they are the victim of medical or healthcare identity theft after adding you to their healthcare plan.

Contact your provider if you receive bills for medical services you never had or calls from debt collectors about medical expenses you owe. Keep your healthcare information safe and secure.

Step 7. Be wary if someone calls or emails with offers for "discount" or "free" health services or products. They typically require you to provide sensitive information and your health plan ID number.

Medical identity thieves may pretend to work for an insurance company, doctors' offices, clinic, or pharmacy to try to trick you into revealing sensitive information.

Step 8. Ghosted! It's called "ghosting" because it can take up to six months for financial institutions, credit-reporting bureaus and the Social Security Administration to register death records.

Criminals have plenty of time to steal identities of loved ones and to rack up charges. Make sure to report the death of your partner or loved ones to Social Security, major credit bureaus, department of motor vehicles, and financial institutions.

Send certified copies of death certificates by certified mail with return receipt.

Step 9. Tax time! Try to file your taxes early to beat out the cybercriminal. Tax Identity Theft happens when someone uses your Social Security number to get a tax refund or a job.

If your e-file return was rejected as a duplicate, you know that you may be a victim of tax-related identity theft. Do not wait to file your taxes.

Thursday Takeaways:

Your most special occasions and your darkest days do not get a free pass from cybercriminals and scammers.

The crooks are more likely to strike when you are distracted, and your guard is down. Maintaining a healthy amount of paranoia at all times is part of developing a strong human firewall.

Hoping for the best but plan for the worst in all areas of your life will help protect you, loved ones and those crown jewels we keep talking about.

As much as you want to share a joyous occasion be sure you only share with the people who you would invite into your own home.
The age-old adage misery loves company is true, but a public display of sadness will hopefully bring out the best in your support group but is also likely to attract the hordes of malicious actors.

Bad guys don't give us any slack when life throws us a curveball or a party. An important part of building your human firewall is making sure the bad guys always have a tough time, so tough they give up, move on to someone else or hopefully get busted.

Day 6: Friday

Intro: Scott W. aka "The Freshman"

Its Friday so skip the salad for lunch and go for the extra-large French fries cause its #FryDay. Today we are walking in the shoes (or sneakers) of Scott W. the college guy, fraternity member and future mechanical engineer.

He is attending school full-time, working part-time and enjoying his first taste of freedom and independence away from his family and parents.

Scott grew up with technology and has been using a computer since kindergarten, so tech is embedded in his life.

Electronic Data security

Scotty boy is "connected" and using technology throughout his school days for all his academics and personal schedule management.
He has a laptop, tablet, smartphone and smartwatch which all keep him connected and one or more are always with him or back in his home base (dorm room).

He relies on technology for note taking in the classroom, research in the study hall and everywhere else he ventures during the day.

He knows data backup is important, so he syncs his critical data and contacts to the cloud and has an external hard drive which he uses to back up his files when he is connected to the drive.

A few topics are covered in this scenario:
Data Backup
Encryption
Cloud
Malware

What should Scott be concerned about in this scenario?

Technology is part of all our lives no matter what your goals and current pursuits. Technology devices and gadgets are useful in all walks of life whether you are a student, professional, business owner, retiree, or stay at home parent.

Technology can make our lives easier, but the risks must be considered as part of our personal protection.

The threats and attack surface increases with each device in your technology arsenal and each device will need its own defenses as part of your overall personal security strategy.

Making yourself a time-consuming hard target increases the likelihood bad guys decide to move along to an easier target and decreases your risk of getting hacked.

How can you build your human firewall and avoid making the same mistakes?

Here's how:

Step 1. Bad Browsers! Update and review browser settings on a regular basis. Modern web browsers offer security features such as auto-updates, privacy protection, blocking known malicious websites and warning of unprotected connection.

On a recurring basis, you must review the updates, settings and features to protect privacy and increase security on your web browsers.

This is especially true right after a version upgrade that may offer new features that need to be secured.

Step 2. Leave no data behind! Devices and software such as browsers save almost everything you do to speed up your experience the next time you visit the same website, enter your payment information or login with your username and password.

With these conveniences comes a host of possible threats which outweigh the benefits. Avoid saving passwords and credentials on any devices and configure auto delete or clearing of data when exiting software and services. Never save anything on a device you do not own.

Step 3. Out of sight out of mind! Store backups offsite to avoid a local disaster from destroying your equipment and data.

If you are performing a backup to a nearby server, USB drive or another storage device you are missing an important point of having a backup. You need to store your backups in a separate location to reduce the risk of all your data being destroyed.

A local fire, flood, storm, earthquake or other disasters can wipe out all your data in a single shot if backups are in the same location.

Step 4. Perform test restores of your backup data to confirm all is working as planned. There is nothing worse than a backup restore failing when you need it.

This was a frequent problem in the old days of tape backup (I know, I'm showing my old age again here). Regularly planned test restores can help prevent failures and identify potential configuration errors in your backup strategy.

Step 5. Ball and chain. Lock them up, bolt them down, and hold on tight to those mobile devices. Never leave your devices unattended.

If you need to leave your laptop, phone, or tablet for any length of time, lock it up with a tethered security lock and chain. Physical protection is just as important as your technical controls.

Step 6. Give bad guys the slip when you encrypt! Encrypt all your data at rest and in transit.

Enable encryption of all your devices so if the devices are lost or stolen the data is not accessible. Do the same for backups in the cloud and on local drives.

Step 7. Two-step is not a dance move! Most modern systems and services offer two-step verification which is also called multi-factor, dual-factor and 2fa.

Enabling two-step requires entering an extra pin-code, biometric or security question after your password to access your accounts.

Doing this reduces your risk of unauthorized account access and may prevent a breach if you fall victim to a phishing email or fake website requesting your username and password.

Step 8. Can you spot the fake? Be careful where you download and what you are downloading. When you are searching to download the latest application, movie or song, think twice about where you are downloading it from.

While there are plenty of legitimate sites from which digital content can be downloaded, there are thousands more fake sites loaded with malware and bad intentions.

Step 9. Reduce your Java! No, you don't have to stop drinking coffee! It is crucial to limit which sites should be allowed to run Java in your web browser.

There is a long list of Java security holes and "drive-by downloads" where just visiting websites can cause malware to be downloaded and executed on your computer.

Another option is removing java completely from your computer.

Physical security

Scott is living in campus housing aka student dorms and was assigned a roommate by the school student housing lottery (there is no Jackpot in this lottery).

His new roomy seems like a cool dude and Scott does not spend much time back in the dorm anyway and it's basically just a place he keeps his stuff and sleeps a few hours.

Campus housing security requires students to use keycards to enter the building, but Scott can easily follow another student inside if he forgets his card.

On occasion, he forgets the key to his dorm room, but he has become a semi-professional lock picker and can easily bypass the door lock with a credit card or paperclip.

A few topics are covered in this scenario:
Physical Security
Hardcopy
Door Locks
Tailgating

What should Scott be concerned about in this scenario?

The physical security of your devices and your personal data is just as important as the technical security.

All the expensive security software, complex passwords and privacy screens become useless if someone can easily break into your home, business or walk off with your unlocked laptop while you're at the counter picking-up with skim mocha frappe latte at your local coffee joint.

Your physical assets can be anything that is of value to you or low-tech criminals who may physically burglarize your home or business and high-tech cybercriminals who may hack their way to your assets.

Your physical assets are located in your homes, cars, offices, on your person, storage facilities and more. Physical security is often overlooked in today's world of smart devices and technology but low or no tech theft of physical devices and data may be a lot easier to steal than trying to hack into your computer or crack your password.

How can you build your human firewall and avoid making the same mistakes?

Here's how:

Step 1. Power Off! Shut it down, lock it, log off, or put your computer to sleep before leaving it unattended and idle for a period.

Make sure that your computer requires a secure password to wake up or startup. Turning off your computer when you are not using your Internet connection can significantly reduce your attack surface.

As mentioned earlier, make sure those devices are also encrypted.

Step 2. Don't overlook physical security. Anyone who can physically access the hardware, data and devices can be a threat.

People such as cleaning staff, building maintenance, property managers, roommates and others may have unrestricted physical access to your devices and data.

Physical access allows bad guys to reset devices, connect unauthorized devices, and bypass network perimeter security.

Be sure to keep devices hidden away or if possible locked up in a secure room or location.

Step 3. Breaking up is hard to do but worth it! Breaking up your home, business or dorm room network into two or more segments can boost your security and keep unsecured or compromised devices from becoming a bigger problem.

By segmenting your network, you can keep your smart devices and guests, which may not have the best security in the world, from your sensitive network files and user data.

Network segmentation is not a silver bullet, but it can be a big security boost and slow down attackers.

Step 4. It's in the box! Get a safe, fire-safe or lockbox to store valuables and keep items safe when not in use.

Get a lockbox large enough to fit cash, identification cards and small electronics that can be easily misplaced or stolen.

This is also very important when you share your space with roommates or others have access when you are not there.

Step 5. Monitor your assets "crown jewels" and set up alerts for changes or unauthorized access. There are many ways to monitor your assets and most are included with your services, but you need to configure the alerts yourself.

Everyone reading this book needs to stop right here and immediately go setup alerts on your financial accounts, so you receive a message the moment there is a transaction on any of your accounts.

Another monitoring and alerting system are cameras and CCTV which can also help deter criminals and random opportunists who may be discouraged by a security camera.

Step 6. Idle time! Your laptop, computer, tablet and smartphone should all auto lock after a very short period of idle time.

An unlocked device with email or contacts accessible could provide unauthorized access to your current messages and every old sent and received email, along with the data and attachments in the messages. Keep devices locked when not in use!

Step 7. Say never to saving. Never save sensitive data in web browsers which often save passwords in plain text format and the data can be exported by anyone or malicious process with physical or remote access to the system.

Turn off the save password, autofill form data, save credit card features in browsers.

Step 8. Toss your cookies! Don't underestimate the amount of data in those saved web browser cookies, internet searches, and browsing history.

The information may contain your name, credit card, and passwords which can be exploited by anyone else with physical access to the device or by malware and vulnerabilities due to missing patches.

Step 9. When in doubt pull it out! Be conscientious of what you plug into your computer and devices. If you notice something new connected it may be because someone else put it there.

Malware can be spread through infected USB flash drives, external hard drives, and even CD/DVDs. If you receive promo items in the mail or in a good bag at an event there is a good chance those devices contain malware.

The devices are inexpensive, cheaply made and the supply chain may have poor security practices. Purchase your computer peripheral devices from well-known and trusted name brands and seller sources.

Step 10. Don't be sloppy with hardcopy! Avoid keeping stacks of mail and statements containing sensitive information in plain sight.

If you have not gone paperless or prefer to print electronic statements be sure to secure the documents until shredding.

It is also critical to properly destroy hardcopy data, so dumpster divers cannot use your trash for identity theft or fraud. Get yourself a shredder that turns paper into micro-size confetti.

Step 11. New keys please! If you lose your keys or cannot remember the last time you changed the locks on your front door, now is a great time to check the locks and get new keys.

Try opening your door with a credit card and if successful you need to add a security plate or get a locksmith to secure the door.

If you are a renter be sure to request the landlord replace crappy locks, change the locks and keys when you move in. Physical security often starts at your front door so repeat after me "secure the front door".

Step 12. No piggyback rides! Do not contribute to tailgating and piggybacking threats by letting the bad guys into your apartment building or office building.

Criminals know most people are naturally polite and will hold a door open for someone carrying a few bags or boxes and they use this technique and others to bypass physical security all the time.

Your act of kindness can potentially put your family, co-workers and friends in danger.

Online Dating security

Scotty is single and like many looking to mingle, he is using online dating to meet his match. He is using dating apps and a website specifically created for people with poor cybersecurity hygiene, the site where the breached go to meet "Weakest Link Match Up".

He has been corresponding with a seemingly nice person who claims to work for a popular bank and it just so happens that this potential match has a fantastic opportunity for him to save money with a great promotion on a low-interest rate credit card.

This person even offers to do him a favor and open the account for him before the deadline expires which just happens to be the next few days. She just needs his full name, address and social security number.

A few topics are covered in this scenario:
Social Engineering
Romance Scams
PII (Personally Identifiable Information)
Unsolicited Communications

What should Scott be concerned about here?

Scammers are lurking everywhere, and online dating is a playground for fraudsters. Dating profiles are detailed, contain pictures, location information and provide more than enough personal information for a scammer to fabricate a personality to make a "connection" with the target.

Scammers look for vulnerable people recovering from illness or recent loss of a loved one or divorce.

The scammers will try to take the conversation off the dating site to avoid detection and so the target does not alert the dating site to the malicious activity. A broken heart and going broke may be the outcome if you're not careful with online dating.

How can you build your human firewall and avoid making the same mistakes?

Here's how:

Step 1. Stranger danger! The saying from your childhood is still very useful and should be practiced when using online dating.

You wouldn't tell a stranger where you live, your phone number or your full name so don't do it with strangers on dating sites or apps.

Step 2. You're just too good to be true and I can't take my eyes off you. If someone seems perfect, knows all the right things to say and is quick to drop the "L" word, the red flashing alarms need to go off.

Refrain from getting all doe-eyed when your potential match claims they love you after a couple of emails.

A romantic courtship is not likely in your future and you are about to get ripped off by dating site fraudsters.

Step 3. Prevent a wreck with a background check! Use the internet search engines to do a background check on your potential new Romeo and their tall tales.

Research a few of their claims and stories to see what is fact and what is fiction. Use photo verification sites to check if their profile pictures are real or you're being catfished.

If they look like a model in the photo, it's probably because the scammer ripped off the glamor shot from another website.

Step 4. Free dating services may come at a cost to your privacy. Good luck making sense of the lengthy privacy agreements.

If the service is free, they are making money in other ways from your usage and your information so shell out a few bucks and get the heightened level of privacy and security that is typical of a paid subscription.

Step 5. What is the rush? Deadlines, urgent action, quick to escalate, highly important and other ways of invoking a sense of fear, excitement or urgency is one of the actions of fraudsters.

We all love a good bargain, deals and opportunities to save or make extra mola (money) but don't let your excitement get the best of your good judgment.

Stop and think it through before you separate yourself from your hard-earned money.

Step 6. Save the favors for your next party. Party favors! Did I mention this is also a bad joke book. Beware of people requesting favors that may get you into trouble or arrested and even more so when the people asking for favors are people you never met.

A few common favor requests include the – can you deposit a check (likely a fake check) for me and wire me the money (please keep a few bucks for your troubles) or can you receive a few packages (of probably stolen merchandise or paid for with stolen credit cards).

Do yourself a favor and don't do anyone any favors.

Step 7. Be suspicious of anyone requesting your personal information. Be just as wary of phone calls as you should be of emails asking for personal information.

Consider sending all calls from unknown callers to voicemail and hang up if you are unsure. Even just providing your full name is supplying too much info because now they confirm who you are, your phone number and that you pick up your phone or open unsolicited emails.

Once they know you are a real person they will likely increase their campaign to rip you off.

Digital Wallet security

Scott likes to travel light and carrying a large bulky wallet stuffed with ID cards, keys, credit cards and more is a nuisance and besides, it does not fit in the pocket of his skinny jeans.

To offset the burden of carrying a wallet he prefers using Mobile Payment Apps and a Virtual Wallet on his smartphone.

He enjoys the convenient tap of his phone against checkout line card readers instead of swiping or dipping a card or plunking down cash.

He is not entirely reliant on apps since unfortunately there are times when vendors and merchants cannot process app payments, so he needs to resort back to cash and credit cards.

A few topics are covered in this scenario:
Payment App
Credit Cards
Digital Wallets
Financial Transactions

What should Scott be concerned about in this scenario?

These days there are many payment options for shopping, paying bills and making all sorts of other financial transactions.

Cold hard cash no longer reigns king in the world of financial transactions and other options often offer reward programs, member discounts, low-interest rates, and convenience.

The list of payment options is growing each year with cash, checks, debit cards, credit cards, mobile wallets, payment apps, cryptocurrency, gift cards, banking apps, and online banking rounding up a lengthy list.

Each type of payment option has its own security pros and cons, mobile wallets use methods such as encryption and tokenization to mask payment card account numbers when you pay.

One thing is true with each cyber bank heist and attack on big financial institutions come new lessons learned and new defenses, making it more difficult for criminals.

Cybercriminals seeking weaker targets are shifting their sights toward individuals and small businesses which typically have fewer security resources and are more vulnerable.

How can you build your human firewall and avoid making the same mistakes?

Here's how:

Step 1. Transformer! Adding payments apps and banking apps to your smartphone transforms it into a completely new asset that requires a higher level of protection.

A lost or compromised phone becomes the equivalent of a lost wallet which in the wrong hands may provide access to your identity, financial information and your contacts.

Treat your phone with the same level of protection you would provide your wallet that is packed with money, credit card and identification.

In other words, do not leave it out in plain sight and in arm's length of grab and go thieves.

Step 2. Get an alert before you get hurt! Nothing hurts more than a swift kick in the wallet. Every one of the electronic financial payment services and systems offer alerts.

Setup your security alerts to receive notifications when there's any transaction or unusual activity on your accounts.

Regularly review and update your alerts and consider adding both a mobile number and email address for alerts, so there is a backup if one is not working or has been compromised.

Step 3. Don't be an Ass! You can't spell password without ass and you're an ass if you don't use complex passwords and unique credentials for all your financial accounts.

Also, as an added precaution, make it a habit of changing your password at least once a year or immediately after any type of breach or identity theft.

Review app security settings on a regular basis and call customer support for assistance adding new security features.

Step 4. If you're wise there won't be a surprise! I love pleasant surprises as much as the next person, just not surprises in my bank account.

Monitor transactions and periodically review your statements for errors or unauthorized activity.

Make it a habit of doing it at least once a month, even if you have not initiated a transaction and don't expect activity on your account.

Step 5. Nothing funny about messing with my money! Cold hard cash, gold bars, and your stash of silver dollar coins all need physical protection.

A fireproof safe, safety deposit box, or on your person can help prevent physical theft of your tangible monies.

Be sure to keep an inventory of locations, total amounts and others (including third-parties and other apps) with authorized access to your financial assets.

Step 6. Built-in protection! Credit cards have significant fraud protection built in, but some payment methods don't.

Also, credit cards are insured, so use it rather than your debit card. Know the payment options when you are making purchases.

Some credit card purchases may also include additional protection and warranty on the purchase at no extra charge, so you can feel guilt-free when you waive offers for extended warranty by the manufacturer or salesperson.

Step 7. Don't be late with an update! Keep your mobile wallet, banking apps and payments apps all updated.

New security features and bug fixes are released on a regular basis and will help protect your financial information and assets.

Also, review security features and add the extra multi-factor or app pin code to secure the systems further.

Step 8. Avoid saving or sharing your credit card information with websites. I know it's so convenient and I sympathize so if truly necessary only save the credit card information on trusted websites that you frequently use.

Try creating a list of the websites where your credit card information is saved and remember breaches are inevitable!

Online Marketplace security

Scott is active on social networking and recently started using several free online marketplaces and apps to buy and sell second hand school books, old computers, tech gadgets and other items he no longer utilizes.

He made several sales and purchases and while most have been online transactions, a few have been local face to face dealings.

The online marketplaces and auctions seem like a great way to save money and to make some quick cash.

A few topics are covered in this scenario:
Dark Web
Online Auctions
Marketplaces
Transactions

What should Scott be concerned about in this scenario?

Selling items or the old junk you no longer use or buying repurposed "used" items can be a great way to make and save money.

Online marketplace and auction services are used by millions of people which creates a great opportunity for sellers and shoppers but also attracts the attention of criminals, scammers and increases the likelihood there will be a few bad apples in the bunch.

Always make safety the highest priority in your wheeling and dealing.

How can you build your human firewall and avoid making the same mistakes?

Here's how:

Step 1. Safety before money! When buying or selling safety should be the highest priority in the transaction.

Losing a device or cash is bad but better than something far more valuable such as your identity or life. If you are making a face-to-face transaction make sure it takes place in a high traffic public place during daytime hours such as a shopping center.

Verify the other person's information and identity. Do not go alone, bringing a friend along will greatly reduce the risk during the transaction.

Step 2. Stay private! Use private browsing to limit tracking of your usage and personal information. Use private browser mode when you're looking to make new purchases such as a car, airfare, hotel booking or any other online purchase.

Private browsing attempts to block web tracking so the websites such as shopping, airlines and hotels can't learn about your purchase plans, travel itinerary, desired dates and other bookings.

The sites use this info to serve up all those clever ads that just magically appear right after your recent search.

Step 3. Freedom isn't free and the same goes for "free services". There is a hidden cost to free and it's typically at a cost to your privacy.

Using free software, apps and services you may be giving permission or unknowingly authorizing access to your personal data and usage as you quickly click through the privacy statement.

If it's free your usage is probably being tracked and sold to data miners and marketers.

Step 4. Just say no! Do not give apps permission to access location, address book, camera or photos on your devices.

Review the privacy settings and deactivate access to unnecessary devices or services such as the microphone, camera, location and notifications.

Disregard the lame warnings that blocking may break some app features and only activate for when you need the permissions enabled but immediately deactivate.

Step 5. No new friends! Just because someone offered to buy your old textbook or TV does not make them friendship material or connection worthy on social networking and it may be a trick to get closer to your other connections who have more private settings.

Unfriend and unfollow unknown social accounts of people you do not know in the real world. Assume if someone messages you who hasn't done so in a while, it is likely a malicious message, such as your friend's account may have been hacked.

Step 6. Spycams! Any used laptop, phone, tablet, video recorder or cameras could be a potential spycam.

Scammers can easily hide keyloggers, remote access trojans (RAT), and other malware to steal your data or record whatever is in front of the camera lenses.

Consider the risk that cameras and other devices could have been programmed as a spying device before being sold.

Step 7. Fake R&R! You cannot always trust the ratings and reviews of products and sellers in online marketplaces. Watch out for reviews that are too positive and lack details of personal experience or opinion.

Some sites and apps allow reviewers to be compensated for ratings which creates another conflict of interest and may create dishonest reviews.

Be sure to check the sources of reviews and the app or sites review policy before you assume a seller or product is safe.

Step 8. Read the fine print! Review the privacy and security settings on apps, websites, and other services you use to ensure they are at your comfort level for information sharing and usage monitoring.

Free is never free when it comes to apps, websites and services. Access to email, contacts list, geolocation, call logs, photos, and more are common but some access sensitive data for advertising reasons.

Step 9. Dead end! Exit scams continue to make money for shady sellers and marketplaces. Online marketplaces may hold transaction monies in escrow until buyers and sellers are satisfied with the transaction before transferring the money.

The escrow is supposed to add a level of security to the transaction, but there have been cases when the online marketplace disappears with all the escrow money. Scamming online sellers may advertise products and collect money without products to sell or intention to deliver anything.

Once they are confronted or called out they disappear and turn up under a new name. Avoid dark web markets and make sure you only deal with reputable marketplaces, sellers and buyers.

Step 10. Malvertisement! Advertisements and ads on legitimate marketplace websites can be compromised and contain malware or redirect you to a malicious site.

Many popular larger websites allow third-party marketing and advertisements. The third-party pipeline can be compromised with advertisements containing malware or embedded viruses.

Websites are working to stop the malicious ads but keeping computer software patched and locking down browser settings will help the issue but there are no guarantees.

Step 11. Sold-out! Online scammers know fans will pay a premium for sold out concerts and events. Do not let the excitement of getting tickets to a sold-out show overcome your better judgment.

Tickets are easy to counterfeit and some of the preferred payment methods have no recourse or protection. Only purchase tickets from a reputable source, company or from the venue.

Step 12. How much is that puppy in the window. Man's and woman's best friend are also one cybercriminals best scams. The internet puppy for sale scam is a very profitable scam for the bad guys.

They create fake puppy sale websites and social media profiles with clever gimmicks such as my family dog just had all these cute puppies and we need to find homes, please help, and lots of adorable puppy pictures.

Go visit your local animal shelter and rescue a pup to avoid the scams.

Friday Takeaways:

Data data everywhere but I have no time to care because I have a date tonight with someone from "Weakest Link Match Up".

I'm sure a lot of readers wouldn't mind having Scott's life, but the truth is we already do, hopefully minus the college debt.

We all have the same data sprawl and security challenges of digital and physical data and information. We give out information, never take it back and lose track of where it lives as we move on.

Our information lives on after we move to the next dating site, online shopping, financial app, physical devices and locations.

Maintaining inventory of data, services and locations it lives can help manage the data sprawl and reduce your personal attack surface.

Making yourself a smaller attack surface or hard target for bad guys is part of building your strong human firewall.

Day 7: Saturday

Introducing: Doctor D. aka "The Professional"

Its Saturday and after a long week you deserve a boozy brunch #Saturdaze. Before we go meet our squad for a bottomless bloody Mary brunch lets meet our small business owner and board-certified dental professional Dr. Diaz.

The good doctor recently expanded his dental practice which includes several locations and a small army of dental assistants, hygienist, and operations support staff.

The business is doing well thanks to their monthly newsletters, social media campaign and website which also includes a customer (patient) portal for making appointments, tracking visits and communicating with the office. Dr. D and his patients are all smiles and no cavities.

Business Computer security

Dr. D named his dental practice "Happy Smiles" and he is smiling because of the growth of his business. With the growth, he has hired several full-time staffers and engaged several third-party services providers to help manage the business.

He has a local technology firm manage the business computers and network, but they charge hourly for time and material, so Dr. D has the office manager to help with basic tech support like setting up employee login credentials.

There are currently more employees than computers, so the staff share computers until new upgrades are purchased. The new employees share the same login credentials while they wait for the office manager to set up more accounts.

The staff accounts are also a local admin account, so they can install software, patches and updates without contacting tech firms.

A few topics are covered in this scenario:
Least Privilege Access
Separation of Duties
Ransomware
Superusers

What should Dr. D be concerned about in this scenario?

Security isn't just a technology challenge. It's also a resource challenge for smaller organizations that can't afford the security operations support necessary in today's threat-filled world.

Employees and owners wear many hats in small businesses which can create more errors and increase the attack surface if one of them is breached.

A breached account with superuser access or elevated privileges may provide an attacker with access to the crown jewels and much more.

How can you build your human firewall and avoid making the same mistakes?

Here's how:

Step 1. Day by Day! Use a day-to-day account with limited privileges instead of an administrator or superuser account for everyday computing.

You may only need to use administrator level access when installing new software and changing system configurations.

Running your computer as an administrator may leave your computer vulnerable to security risk. You will be much more susceptible to ransomware, adware and spyware when using a super-user account for daily web browsing and accessing email.

Step 2. Deactivated! Any non-work-related software and services should be disabled on business and office computers.

This will help prevent anyone such as employees, cleaning staff, or visitors from browsing to personal email, clicking a malicious link and downloading ransomware to business computers.

Step 3. Inventory control! Maintaining a hardware and software inventory will help identify suspicious activity, unauthorized applications and rogue employees on your network and devices.

It will also help keep track of older devices and applications nearing the end of life which you should retire before they become a threat due to lack of vendor support for security updates.

Step 4. Do not be a historian of old operating systems. Running software past its EOL (End of Life) means your obsolete OS (Operating System) will no longer receive software updates from Windows Update, including security updates that can help protect your computer from harmful viruses and malware.

Your computer will likely be vulnerable and an easy target for malware and hackers.

Step 5. Let's get physical, physical, physical. Seriously listening to Pat Benatar's "Let's Get Physical" is a great reminder to restrict physical access to devices such as printers.

Also limit access to parts of the printer such as the internal hard drive (on larger devices), external USB ports and SD card slots.

Physical access can easily allow a malicious actor an opportunity to exploit your systems.

Step 6. Put a halt to the default passcode! Seriously everyone with physical access to your printer can do a quick web search to locate your default passcode of 1111 or admin.

This is also assuming there is even the most basic security in the first on the device. Change passcode/pin codes as soon as possible and do not write the code on the device.

Use your password vault to store the password securely.

Step 7. FaxPloited! It's hard to imagine we are still discussing fax machines today but there are still plenty of these devices connected to networks which makes them a target.

The problem becomes more challenging because the technology has not changed much in 30 years and security is an afterthought.

Faxed data is not secure and is not encrypted, data can be intercepted just like any tapped phone line. The best defense is stop using the old technology.

Step 8. Deactivate! Turn off unnecessary systems, services and features that you do not use. You may not even have to connect your printer to the wireless network if it is connected to a single computer by a cable.

Turn off network settings and wireless settings you are not using. If you have a network printer there are a host of other services that you should also deactivate if they are not in use.

It is best to contact the manufacturer support or a printer tech support pro for assistance.

Step 9. Trust is a must! You should never download and install software from random websites you don't know and trust.

Be sure to scan any files or software with a good antivirus program. Be sure to obtain software from legitimate sources and use custom install settings to prevent "bundling" of additional unwanted programs with legitimate software.

Step 10. Surprise! If you don't like surprises, enable the monitoring and alert features on your hardware and devices.

Spend time on configuring the types of alerts and frequency. I suggest at least enabling monitoring and alerting on software updates, configuration changes, reboots, errors and when new devices connect to the network.

This will help identify malicious activity and rogue devices on your home and business network.

Step 11. Reduce the juice or you might be a drive-by victim! You should lower the power on your wireless radio so it's not broadcasting down the street or to the parking lot of your office.

The local cyber-goons are likely doing drive-by wardriving attacks to map out all the local wireless networks to use as recruits for their next botnet army they plan to use to take down your favorite streaming video site.

Keeping the wireless router in the middle of your home or office also reduces the radius of your radio signal.

Step 12. Don't get flashed! Some websites still use Adobe Flash to display content and media.

Attackers can also use the security flaws in Flash to run malicious software on your computer and gain access to your system.

If you must use Flash on your computer, keep the software up to date and enable "click to play" in your web browser to block automatic flash plugin activation.

Public Relations security

Dr. D's is busy running the business and working 60+ hours a week, so he has no time to manage marketing and does not have the budget to hire a public relations firm.

When his team of office managers and assistants volunteered to take on the task he was thrilled to offload the responsibility. They have done a fantastic job with social media marketing campaigns, newsletters and new website content.

Dr. D did manage the social media and website in the past and he would also send the occasional "dental care tips" email to his client distribution list.

Since he already had the accounts configured, he gave the staff his credentials to use when they took over the marketing reins.

A few topics are covered in this scenario:
Shared Credentials
Audit Trail
Websites
Marketing

What should Dr. D be concerned about in this scenario?

Social media and online marketing can help promote your business and brand, but it can also destroy your reputation and livelihood.

Consider security when developing a marketing strategy that includes training your staff on social media security best practices procedures.

The training and procedures should be easy to understand, give employees the chance to engage, and provide a sense of how important it is to follow the security procedures.

Give employees or vendors the ability to draft posting and distribution material but leave the go live launch button press to a trusted person on your team.

Unique limited access credentials for everyone involved will deter sharing passwords and provide an audit trail of changes and activity which can be very useful if there is ever a breach.

How can you build your human firewall and avoid making the same mistakes?

Here's how:

Step 1. Document and regularly review who or what has access to your assets "crown jewels" to reduce unauthorized access and theft of your assets.

Remember your reputation and brand is one of your assets and should be treated like gold.

Step 2. Out of sight! Restrict access to the non-public section of your website. Limit who can access and change your data and services.

Review access controls on a regular basis and watch out for the share with everyone and public settings. Most of the newsworthy cloud data breaches are caused by user errors accidentally enabling public sharing.

Step 3. Sync may get you sunk. Syncing the data from your computer, phone or tablet to the cloud or social media sites may seem like a great idea until you accidently sync sensitive data (or pictures) or you sync malware infected data.

Mixing personal accounts with business data may unintentionally sync sensitive data to your personal accounts or accounts you share with family members.

Step 4. Unapproved! Set up an approval procedure and controls for publishing marketing and news distribution.

Have an approval process and procedure that includes reviewing and signoff by more than one person to reduce errors, prevent unapproved information sharing and unauthorized posts.

Step 5. Audit trail mix. Everyone involved should have their own accounts and credentials so there is an audit trail and accountability throughout the workflow.

This also helps prevent sharing credentials and unauthorized escalated privileges.

Step 6. Train your brain. General cybersecurity training for all levels of staff can save the company from costly breach recovery.

Also, equally as important is job specific cyber awareness training for cybercriminal targets such as Human Resources, Marketing, Accounting, Executives and Finance departments.

Step 7. Don't reuse passwords on personal and work accounts. Organizations of all sizes are under attack by cybercriminals and if your company is breached your personal data is likely to be stolen.

Criminals will attempt to reuse the same credentials on popular services and websites.

Step 8. Paparazzi! You need your brand and reputation monitored like a celebrity followed by a pack of the paparazzi.

Brand, website and social media monitoring tools and services can help monitor for unauthorized updates, posts, and outages.

Your online presence is your most active communication channel you have and must be monitored and protected.

Step 9. Least privy! The practice of least privileged access can save your butt when you get reeled in by an enticing link or file attachment.

Using an everyday user account with the least amount of privileges necessary to perform basic computing may prevent malware installs.

A malicious actor or process can exploit your permissions to access your computer peripherals or services to do harm and steal information.

It may also prevent basic human errors or a quick to click error from installing malware or giving a process access to your camera.

Trade Show security

Dr. D is a member of several dental associations and peer groups. He also regularly attends conferences and trade shows.

He has decided to sponsor a table at an upcoming trade show and have his staff hand out promotional items such as "Happy Smiles" branded toothbrushes, USB drives, phone charges and rechargeable USB flashlights and host a raffle for free dental services for one year.

He has his team distribute the information in a newsletter and add the raffle signup to the social media account to reach an even larger audience.

A few topics are covered in this scenario:
Raffle Scams
Promotional Items
Free Swag
Evil Twins

What should Dr. D be concerned about in this scenario?

Trade Shows, events and large gatherings of people, technology and sensitive data attract hackers like sharks to blood in the water.

Goody bags full of gadgets, pens, and stress squeeze balls are a novelty at tradeshows, conferences and business events but the sources of the items are concerning.

While you are trying to network and develop your brands, the cybercriminals and scammers are also hard at work using free swag and gadgets to deliver the malware that is piggybacking on the devices.

The inexpensive and mass-produced tech gadgets may contain malicious software and unsuspecting recipients may be at risk if they use the devices.

How can you build your human firewall and avoid making the same mistakes?

Here's how:

Step 1. Close your backdoor! Hackers will always take advantage of human errors, poor judgment and open backdoors.

Before you take your devices on the road make sure all your software is patched, disable any unnecessary services, update your security software (antivirus), encrypt your devices and backup important data. Prepare for the worst-case scenario such as a stolen or hacked device.

Step 2. There is no such thing as a free lunch! Dropping your business card in our fishbowl to win a free lunch is more like losing your mind with all the spam and telemarketing calls you will receive once we resell your information.

Do not give away your information for a free lunch, donut, cup of coffee or anything else. Protect your identity and personal information like it's a suitcase full of cash.

Step 3. Yeah, goodie bags! Free swag and goodie bags are great but watch out for the electronic gadgets that are included.

Those USB storage thumb drives, cell phone chargers, and others are made as cheap as possible and there have been cases where they contain malware and spyware so toss them out.

Step 4. Supply chain gang! There have been countless incidents where legitimate sources and businesses unknowingly distributed malware on devices intended for distribution of legitimate data, marketing or promotion.

Purchasing cheap computer peripherals from untrusted sources may introduce malware or spyware into your device or network.

Step 5. Phys Ed! Put all that you have learned about physical security into practice at events.

Use privacy screens on computers and laptops, idle devices should quickly lock when not in use, security chains and teethers for devices and do not leave devices unattended.

Also, consider using travel or loaner computers for events which should not contain any sensitive data and can be reformatted (wiped clean).

Step 6. Bring your own! Bring your own internet connection to events to avoid connecting to the shared public wireless networks.

Scammers (and competitors) set up malicious wireless networks that impersonate the legitimate networks in hopes that unsuspecting attendees connect to the network.

Once you are connected the scammers can eavesdrop on your traffic, intercept credentials and passwords. Bring your own hotspot to avoid the evil twins.

Step 7. Registered for fraud! Scammers have great timing and just as upcoming trade show and event dates approach the fraudsters start requesting fees.

Scammers make big bucks impersonating familiar trade shows and popular industry events by requesting attendee ticket charges, booth fees and special offers for VIP access.

Before you pay for that pricey all-inclusive VIP pass contact the event directly to confirm it is legit and if you do pay, use a credit card for extra fraud protection.

Smart Office security

Dr. D has decided to update security in his offices by adding new security cameras that allow him to monitor the offices from anywhere using his smartphone.

He is also adding new features for customers such as smart coffee machines, guest wireless, smartphone charging stations, smart televisions, guest computers, guest color printing, and Bluetooth speakers to allow visitors to stream their personal playlist music in dental rooms.

All he needs now is a few freelancers, beer taps and snacks to make his office into a hip coworking incubator space.

A few topics are covered in this scenario:
Guest Wi-Fi
Wireless Encryption
Smart Devices
Security Cameras

What should Dr. D be concerned about in this scenario?

Smart devices and high-tech gadgets are in every home and office now. The devices are helpful and entertaining but also present a new and growing security threat.

Any smart device connected to the company wireless network, authorized or otherwise, can present a risk to the network. Your company's next major security breach may come from a device as seemingly innocent as the coffee maker.

Introducing new technology also introduces new threats and vulnerabilities. Before rolling out any new technology, you should review the potential new risks.

How can you build your human firewall and avoid making the same mistakes?

Here's how:

Step 1. MAC Attack! This Mac Attack won't send you running to the nearest McD's for two beef patties, special sauce, lettuce and cheese.

You should always use network access controls (NAC) and MAC address filters to block unauthorized devices from connecting to your network. Permitting only trusted devices to connect will prevent unauthorized devices from connecting to your private or business network.

Step 2. Get Boosted! Give your network security a boost by enabling all the built-in security features.

Most modern firewalls and security appliances are packed with security features (firewall, intrusion protection, encryption, web filtering) that may come disabled fresh out of the box.

Contact a professional of customer support to make sure you get the most security out of your hardware and security devices.

Step 3. Defaulted! Change the default passwords and codes on all smart devices. Anyone on the same network or with physical access can easily bypass the security of the devices with the default passwords.

It is also very easy to search the internet and find the default password for any device.

Step 4. No Interlopers! Don't let a poorly configured open guest wireless network allow strangers to take a free ride on your network.

You should add a passcode to the guest network access so that strangers within range can't use your network any time they like and potentially gain access to other devices on your network.

Periodic password changes are a must so set a reminder to change the passcode every month.

Step 5. High-tech Spy-tech! Any devices with a microphone and camera can potentially be turned into a spying device.

Laptops, tablets, smartphones and even smart TV's have the multimedia hardware to be hijacked and transformed into a listen and video recording device.

Cover up cameras that are not in use and disable unused microphones.

Step 6. Slice and dice! Slice up the network or use different devices for each network. Be sure to have a business only trusted network for company devices, a guest/visitor network and a network for smart devices and untrusted devices.

Separating devices and networks will reduce the threat when a device or network are breached, or an infected device connects to the network.

E-Communications security

Dr. D and his staff receive a lot of emails, text messages and phone calls each day and recently noticed an uptick in the number of cold calls, telemarketers, text message spam, fake emails and attachments.

The doctor himself was the victim of ransomware in the past when he mistakenly opened a malicious file attachment.

Dr. D requested his technology service provider assist and they recommend upgrading the antivirus and adding a new email spam filter.

A few topics are covered in this scenario:
Staff Training
Web Filtering
Defense in Depth
Software Updates

What should Dr. D be concerned about in this scenario?

You cannot trust email, caller ID, unsolicited calls and even text messages from friends, family and other trusted senders.

Current technology has made it very easy for malicious actors to craft realistic looking emails and calls using internet calling and texting services and exploited email protocols and systems.

It is easier than ever for cybercriminals to abuse these services to impersonate and use email, caller ID spoofing to make incoming messages look like they are coming from a legitimate or known phone number or email address.

Attackers also use special techniques to hijack and intercept calls and important text messages like multi-factor codes or one-time passcodes.

Security tools and systems are not 100% accurate so there will always be false positives and items that slip through the defenses.

How can you build your human firewall and avoid making the same mistakes?

Here's how:

Step 1. Don't trust caller ID. Just because your caller ID displays a phone number or name of a legitimate person or company you may recognize, it does not guarantee the call is really coming from that source.

It's very easy for the bad guys to spoof caller ID. If the name of your bank shows on an unexpected inbound caller ID don't pick up the call, instead call your bank at the phone number on your debit or credit card.

Step 2. Don't call me, I will call you! Ask to call back and compare the number to the company website or information you have in your address book.

Tell callers you will call them back then verify that the company is legitimate.

Step 3. Learn to politely say go F yourself. Just say no. A legitimate company will never pressure you or use scare tactics to force you to supply sensitive information or access to your device.

Never provide credit card information or other private information to anyone who calls you. Politely say F off!

Step 4. Found you! Do you really need your friends, family and stalkers popping up everywhere you go?

The locator service functions can be a nightmare for multiple reasons that probably deserve their own independent book.

Imagine you smartly deactivated the geolocator services, but your idiot friend still uses the services and just tagged you in a picture which then identifies your location as a baseball game when you just called out sick from work, your boss will not be happy.

That situation is not that bad but could be very dangerous when you consider stalkers and cyber-stalkers may abuse the locator services to find your home, work or other places you frequent.

Step 5. End Calls! The do not call list does work if you take a minute to register your phone number.

Adding your number to the FTC's national do not call register will reduce telemarketer calls and the annoying dead silence when predictive dialing causes abandoned calls.

Step 6. Secure your phone accounts! Securing your accounts comes up in several areas of this book but this item is especially important.

Your phone company's customer portal website needs to be secured with very strong and unique passwords and ideally also has multi-factor enabled.

Besides having your home address and billing information many of the phone service provider web portals features include access to call history, voicemail, text messages, contact list and some even allow you to send messages from the portal.

The list of bad things cybercriminals can do with a compromised phone account is endless.

Saturday Takeaways:

Business owners have double trouble when it comes to cybersecurity. As does every professional who lives the dual technology life of managing both professional work and personal technology devices and services.

It is very common to have separate devices and service accounts for professional and personal systems which may seem like double the work but worth the extra security.

The security or convenience debate is a waste of time and energy that is better spent building your human firewall. Separating professional and personal technology will significantly reduce the impact of a breach because of the limited access and separation of duties.

Cyber awareness training for employees and creating a top-down cybersecurity culture will increase buy-in from staff and help secure the business.

As we know breaches are inevitable and decreasing the impact of the eventual data breach is part of building your human firewall.

Closing

Congratulations you survived seven whole days of Human Firewall Building and by now you are likely exhausted after several sleepless nights caused by nightmares filled with evildoers and cybercriminals.

It is understandable to feel angry, frustrated and even helpless when thinking about the monumental task of building and maintaining your human firewall.

Now is the time to reach down inside yourself for that spark that can ignite your fire(wall) that roars "I can do this, and I will do this". If you cannot find that spark or do not want to build it alone, the next best thing is the buddy system or even better make it a group event with friends, family and coworkers because everyone needs human firewall building.

Pay it forward by finding new ways to make cybersecurity a daily topic of conversation that includes current events and tips to reduce the threats.

You may enjoy cybersecurity and human firewall building so much you consider a career change and with the estimated 2+ million unfilled jobs, we could really use your help. With enough time, energy and focus anything is possible, best of luck Human Firewalls!

Glossary

2FA	Two-factor authentication adds an extra layer of security and requires two types of authentication to verify identity
App	A program installed and run on mobile devices and smartphones
App Store	An online store to purchase and download free apps
Backdoor	A secret method to bypass the normal authentication on a system
Biometric	Used to measure a physical characteristic such as a fingerprint to confirm identity
Bitcoins	Digital crypto currency used for online transactions
Bits	A basic or small amount of data
Blog	An online personal website that contains comments and reflections provided by a writer
Bluetooth	A shortwave wireless network technology commonly used in smartphones and mobile devices
Botnet	An army of compromised zombie computers or devices controlled by a malicious actor and used to attack other networks, services and providers
Breach (Data)	Unauthorized access to nonpublic information and systems
CCTV	Close circuit television also called

	security cameras
CISA	An ISACA Certified Information Security Auditor
CISM	An ISACA Certified Information Security Manager
CISO	Chief Information Security Officer
CISSP	An (ISC)2 Certified Information Systems Security Professional
Clickbait	A link designed to entice users to click
Crown Jewels	The most prized assets of an individual or organization
CTO	Chief Technology Officer
Dark web	A hidden part of the internet that is not indexed by common search engines and web browsers
DDoS	A flood of unwanted traffic resulting in overwhelming traffic to a website or service
Defense in Depth	A concept of adding multiple layers of security defenses to deter, catch and prevent attacks
Dictionary Attack	A password cracking attack that uses words from the dictionary to guess passwords
Digital Footprint	The traceable online activities, actions, contributions and communications that are trackable on the internet or on devices
Encryption	A process of making information unreadable without a special key or passcode
End of Life	The end of a products usefulness or

(EOL)	support by manufacture
Evil twin	A malicious wireless network access point that impersonates a legitimate network
Firewall	A network security system that monitors and filters inbound and outbound traffic
Flash	A software platform developed by Adobe Systems
Geotag	Geographical information added to photos, websites, messages and others that is used to pinpoint the location of the information or person
GPS	Global Positioning System is a satellite-based navigation system for used directions and tracking
Hacker	Someone who uses technical skills to gain unauthorized access to computers
Hacktivists	Hackers who break into networks and websites to convey a political or social message
HTTP	Hypertext Transfer Protocol is the underlying protocol of the world wide web for directing webservers and web browsers
HTTPS	Secure version of HTTP that uses transportation layer security (TLS) encryption
Intellectual Property (IP)	Intangible creations such as "secret sauce", trade secrets, patents and trademarks
IoT	Internet of Things are everyday

	objects connected to the internet and able to communicate over a network and the internet
Java	A computer programming language created to run on all platforms and operating systems
Malvertising	A malicious advertisement that spreads malware
Malware	A malicious program designed to cause damage to computers and networks
Man-in-the-Middle	A MitM attack occurs when an eavesdropper intercepts a communication and relays the information, so the parties are unaware of the listening
MFA	Multi Factor Authentication requires more than one authentication method to validate access
Morris worm	One of the first publicized computer worm viruses distributed by internet in 1988
Operating System (OS)	The underlying computer software that manages the hardware and software resources
Passcode	A secret sequence of characters for gaining access to a system or services
Phishing	An attempt typically a fake email to obtain credentials, credit cards and personal information
Plugin	A software component that adds a feature to an existing application
Ransomware	A type of malware that encrypts data

	and demands a ransom payment typically in cryptocurrency for the encryption key
RAT	Remote Access Trojan allows an attacker remote takeover of a compromised computer
Rootkit	A malicious software that allows a remote user elevated access permission to the compromised computer
Shoulder Surfing	A social engineering technique used to physically look over a victim's shoulder to view sensitive information and passwords
SIM Jack	Unauthorized redirection of a victim's subscriber identification module (SIM) to intercept email, calls and messages
Smishing	A malicious text message which typically contains a link to a website or file
Social Bot	SocBots are chat bots on social networks that are typically used to generate messages and following for ideas, accounts and messages
Social Engineer	A con-artist person who uses social manipulation to get people to divulge sensitive information and perform tasks
Spyware	Computer software that collects information without the consent of the user
SSID	A Service Set Identifier is used for

	broadcasting and naming wireless networks
Superuser	An administrative account with full access to all services and resources
Swag	Promotional items or ornamental items
Tagging	Attaching keywords and people to images, websites and postings
Tailgating	Also called Piggybacking occurs when an unauthorized person closely follows a person with authorized physical access to a secure area
TLS	Transport Layer Security is a secure communications protocol that encrypts data in transit
Two-step	Two-step verification is a method of confirming an identity and granting access only after two verification methods are approved
U2	An Irish rock band formed in the mid-1970s and still touring today
Untag	Removing tags connecting a person, place or thing to a picture, website, blog post and video
UPnP	Universal Plug and Play lets networked devices auto discover each other on a wireless network
Virtual Digital Assistant	Software platforms that assists people and perform basic tasks such as reading an email or dialing a phone call
VPN	Virtual Private Networks allow people to communicate data securely

	over the public internet
Worm virus	A computer virus that replicates over the network and spreads to other computers
Zero-Day (0-day)	An unknown and unpatched vulnerability that can be exploited by hackers
Zombie	A computer that has been compromised and is under the control of hackers